"TURNING LIFE'S ~~V~~... ~~S~~"

WHEN LIFE GIVES YOU LEMONS

OPEN A LEMONADE STAND

ELIZABETH W. WILSON

When Life Gives You Lemons, Open a Lemonade Stand
Copyright © 2007 by Elizabeth W. Wilson
Onyx Publishing House
3695F Cascade Road, Suite 1124
Atlanta, Georgia 30331

ISBN-13: 978-0-615-13588-5
ISBN-10: 0-615-13588-9
Wilson, Elizabeth
When Life Gives You Lemons, Open a Lemonade Stand
www.elizabethwwilson.com

Cover Design, Book Design and Printing by
Custom Made For You Graphic Design & Printing
www.custommadeforyou.net

Manufactured and printed in the United States of America

All rights reserved. No part of this publication may be reproduced. Stored in a retrieval system or transmitted in any form by any means electronic, mechanical, photocopying, recording or otherwise without written permission of the publisher.

Dedication

To my father, Pastor Robert C. Williams, and my late mother, Catherine Agee Williams.

To my siblings, Sandra White, Robert Williams Jr., Anita Douglas, and Angela Williams
To my loving husband, C. W. Wilson.
You will always be home to me.

Acknowledgements

I would like to extend my sincere appreciation to those who have aided me in the production of this book. First, the pushers bugged me, shamed me, and would not leave me alone. The biggest pusher, God, gave me the idea for this book seven years ago. He would not let me rest until I wrote the vision and made it plain. He is my inspiration and salvation. I thank him for choosing me to serve in this capacity. To the little pushers, my girlfriends, Antoinette Ball, Roberta Nance, Theresa Johnson, Bernadette Jones, Kathy Holmes-Bass, Shirley Hines, Mary McVay, Martha Gooddine, and Patricia Williams, you encouraged me to do my best and follow my heart. To Adele, my girlfriend in heaven, you look down on me and make me feel special every day.

Next, I want to acknowledge the producers, the individuals with writing and creative expertise that helped me develop a product I am proud to put my name on. To Lacie Williams of Custom Made For You, thanks for your excellent book cover design and layout. To Natalie Keiser and Dee Wallace, thanks for your cold-blooded editing in the past. To Rochele Hirsh, past president of the Atlanta Women's Network, thanks for making me see the possibilities of leadership. To entrepreneur and activist, Jane Fonda, thank you for your support of microenterprise for women in Georgia. Her vision started me on the path of entrepreneurship training.

Finally to the products, the hundreds of entrepreneurs I have had the honor to serve over the last ten years as I developed the lemonade stand concepts, I have highlighted many of the creative businesses that these talented individuals have produced. I am honored and humbled to have been a small part of their lives. I hope this work will continue to light other entrepreneurial flames for years to come.

Table of Contents

Why a Lemonade Stand? 13

Lemons Happen 19

What Not to Do When You Get Lemoned 23

Your Worst Time? Best Time for Business 27

Okay, Now What? Take the E Test 31

Lemon #1: Illness and Disability 39

Lemon #2: Domestic Violence 53

Lemon #3: Incarceration 69

Lemon #4: Debt 81

Lemon #5: Natural Disasters 89

Lemon #6: Your Past 97

Lemon #7: Death 101

Turn Your Woe into Dough 107

Opening a Lemonade Stand Is Easy 111

Biblical Lemonade Stands 119

Lemonaires 123

Lemonade Stands for Everybody! 129

Water

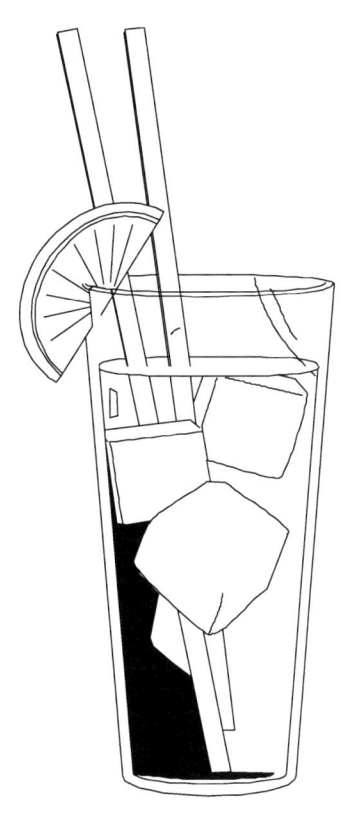

Abundant Natural Resources

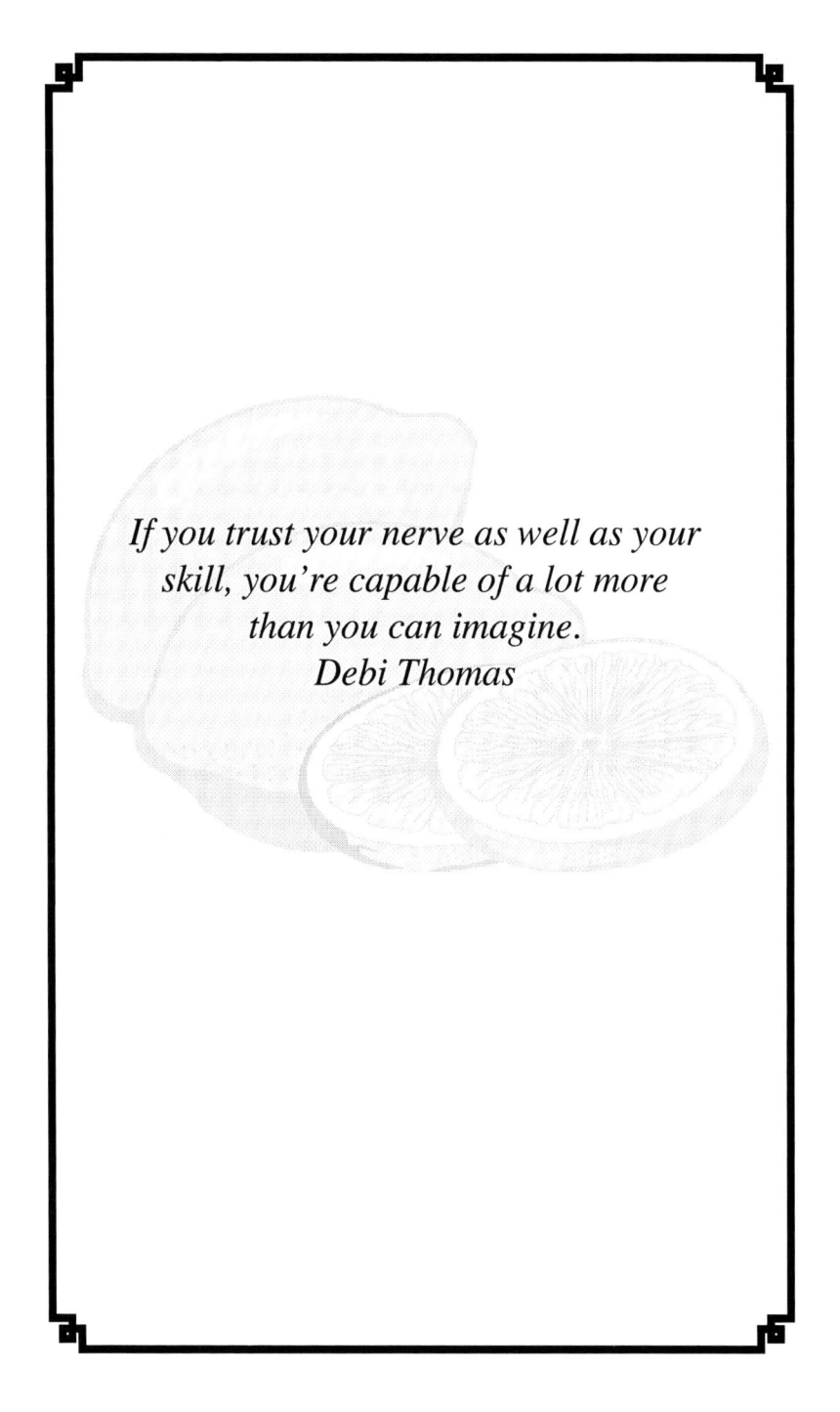

*If you trust your nerve as well as your
skill, you're capable of a lot more
than you can imagine.
Debi Thomas*

Why a Lemonade Stand?

Why lemons? Why lemonade stand? "When life gives you lemons make lemonade." My friend Leslie would use this saying as the new "have a nice day" or, the Christian equivalent, "I'm blessed." Making lemonade seems to be the answer to any bad situation. Yeah … right. After hearing this same statement repeatedly, I started responding, "To make lemonade, you need more than lemons. You need sugar, too." You actually need more than sugar. You need lemons, water, and sugar that are mixed together in the right portions to get true lemonade.

Lemonade is the cool, refreshing summer drink. Even more than iced tea, lemonade is the all-American refresher. It is the little guy of liquid refreshment. Tea, on the other hand, has gone through so many incarnations. There's herbal tea, hot tea, decaffeinated tea, blended tea, chai tea, green tea, Arizona tea, Canadian tea, Chinese tea, and so forth. And don't even get me started with coffee! No, lemonade is the everyman drink, the popular beverage of youngsters, teens, adults, and seniors. It's the answer to any hot day or hot situation. However, even though that idea is refreshing, at the close of the day when you have an empty glass, you only have pulp to show for it.

How can we extend the lemonade vernacular and really make lemons the response to many of life's problems? How can we accept the sour things of life and make them sweeter? How can someone take his or her sour experiences, like lemons, and turn them into refreshing opportunities that expand beyond the pulp? How can you stretch that good feeling beyond a cool drink? Sometimes, we tend to go for the quick fix rather than allow our minds to create an entirely different life scenario from a bad situation.

In the next few chapters, I will take you on a journey to explore some of life's lemons, that is, life's problems, significant issues, and situations. We will see how we can turn them into opportunities. Together, we will explore avenues to turn adventures into ventures. We will pick life's broken pieces and turn them into financial mosaics. We will potentially see the busted and disgusted pieces of our lives as possible business opportunities.

Simply put, a lemonade stand is a better way to turn lemons into something profitable. Lemonade stands are simple. Children fearlessly launch these retail businesses every day! There are different ways you can take your life's lemons and turn them into lemonade stands. You can profit from your pain by turning life's valleys into business ventures. Why do I think you can do it? Others have done the same thing. They turned lemons into lemonade stands, and some have achieved outstanding business results. Successful business enterprises begin in the strangest places. Success grows in the strangest soil. Don't forget that fertilizer produces fruit!
I will help you think of directions that you can turn some of life's challenges into possible business ventures. The ultimate goals of this publication will be to:

- Help you see various ways that life's tragedies can be turned into successful business strategies.
- Share helpful resources that are available to help you start and develop a successful business enterprise.

- Chronicle stories of entrepreneurs who accepted their problems and turned them into profits.
- Encourage you to keep trying to better your life, especially your financial life. Don't give up even when you're down and out.
- Give you "recipes" for successful business development.
- Teach you to start well, develop a working plan, draw on the resources available to you, identify resources for your work and develop SMART (specific, measurable, attainable, realistic, and trackable) goals.
- Share stories of real-life "lemonaires."
- Recognize supportive groups who wish to help you move up and out of those situations you may find yourself stuck in.

Remember, you only need three ingredients to make lemonade: water (abundant natural resources), lemons (sour stuff and icky things), and sugar (sweet man-made resources). You can also use these same ingredients as a guide or a recipe for a successful small enterprise. You identify assets (abundant available tools to help you grow your special talent or skill), acknowledge the difficulties or issues (sour stuff and unmet needs), and focus your talent or business idea (those "sweet" things that makes you unique, that is, your skills, experiences, or markets).

When the right ingredients come together in the right mix, the result is the same. A focused "lemonade stand mentality" can add up to sweet business opportunities. A sweet business adds to your life and does not take away from it. You enjoy doing a sweet business. A sweet business instantly brings pleasure to your life and a smile to your face when you think about it. A sweet business is a good thing that you have added to the world. A sweet business is refreshing!

And that's the way it is.
Walter Cronkite

Lemons Happen

Life's lemons can be anything that comes your way and throws you off track. Life's lemons steal your joy, peace of mind, and vitality. A lemon can knock the wind out of your sails and zap your creativity. Lemons are major distractions like illness, debt, addictions, past experiences, and incarcerations. They steal time, youth, money, and creativity. Time is a limited commodity. Lack of time, time spent, and times wasted are all lemons. Have you ever noticed how the word "lemon" seems to be from the same family of words as demon and omen?

Eventually, all of us get lemoned. We're unexpectedly hit below the belt and thrown off course. Lemons hurt. You don't pick your lemons, but, you can sometimes plant them, grow them, and reap them.

Throughout history, the lemon has been given a pretty bad rap. Lemons could use a good public relations agent. Lemons are associated with bad things. Irreparable appliances are called lemons. Across the country, lemon laws give owners recourse to return cars after multiple attempts at repairs. Anything that refuses to function correctly is called a lemon. Let's look at the lowly lemon and delve a bit into its illustrious past.

The Merriam-Webster Dictionary defines a lemon as: a hybrid citrus tree of cultivated origin. The fruit is used primarily for its juice, though the pulp; rind and zest are also used. Lemon juice is 5 percent citric acid, which gives this fruit a sour taste.

The thorny branches on lemon trees can grow flowers and ripe fruit at the same time. Lemons can be a metaphor for life. They thrive in fertile soils and need ample quantities of sunlight. Lemons are also considered a medicinal fruit. For example, sailors once used lemons to combat scurvy because they provided a large dose of vitamin C. Lemons are preservatives. If sprinkled over other fruit, lemon juice can impede the oxidation process. Lemons can be added in baking goods, squeezed on fish, and used as a marinade for meats.

The Reader's Digest Web site[1] and other popular magazines list several other household uses for lemons.
Lemons can:
- whiten clothing
- remove tough stains on marble
- keep rice from sticking
- clean microwave ovens
- boost laundry detergents
- sanitize hands, polish chrome
- deodorize garbage disposals
- eliminate fireplace odors
- neutralize litter box odors
- refresh cutting boards
- remove underarm stains from clothing
- reduce facial acne
- brighten aluminum
- disinfect wounds.

How can something so bad also be so good? How can something so negative also be used in so many positive, productive ways? It seems as if life gives you lemons, as negative as it may be for a reason, a purpose, also. Lemons can change the course of the meal as they can the course of a life. Their sour juices compliment sweet drinks like tea, flavor candies, cakes, pies and cookies and as an ingredient, it stand quite well on its own. No surprise life gives us lemons; they can take a licking and keep on ticking!

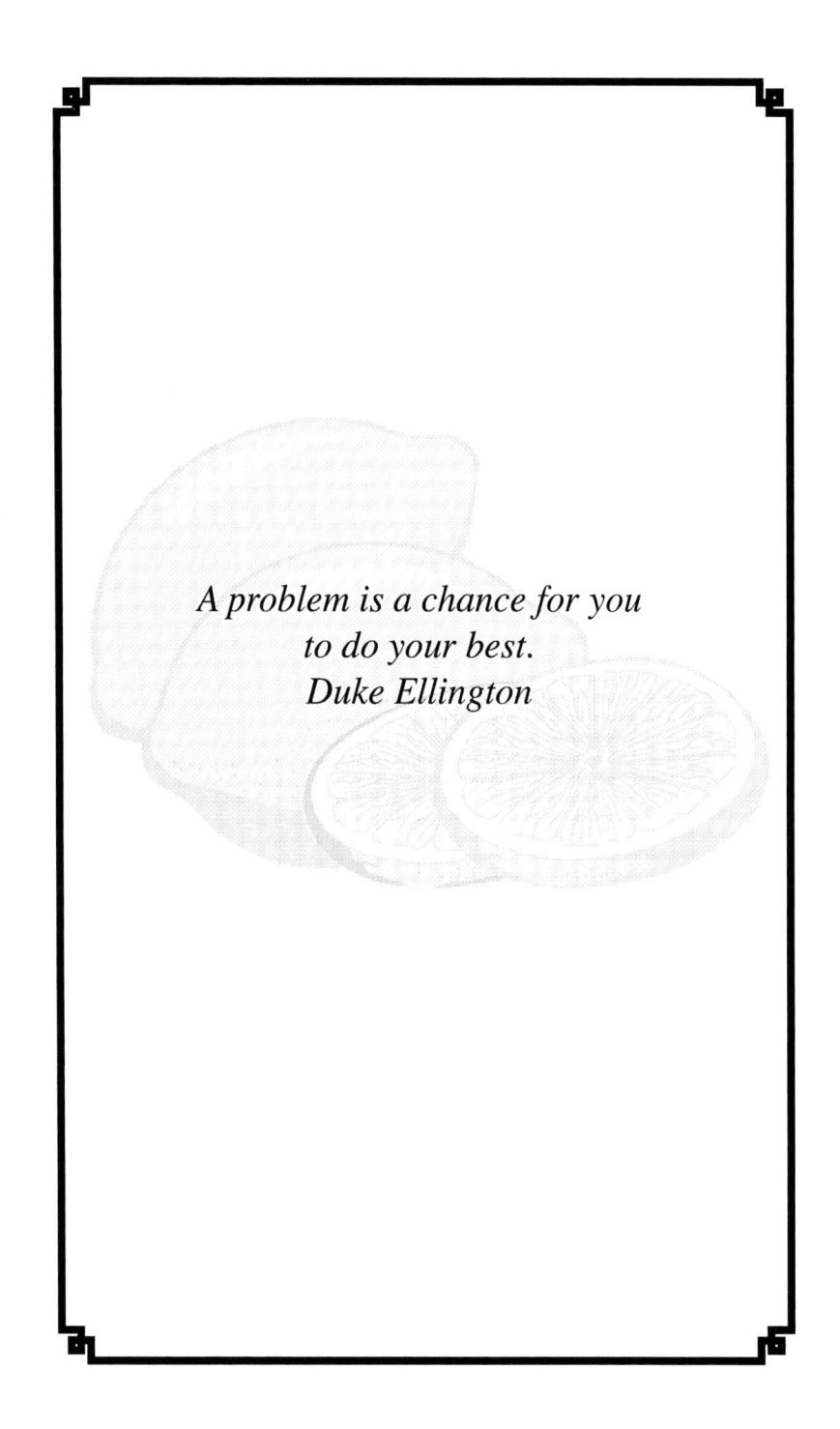

*A problem is a chance for you
to do your best.
Duke Ellington*

What Not to Do When You Get Lemoned

Eventually, all of us get lemoned. All of us face some unexpected, unwanted, uninvited lemon twist that makes everything before it seem rather small. A lemon can be anything that throws you off your life's track. Maybe you were in the wrong place at the wrong time. Maybe you hung out with the wrong crowd. Maybe you were born. Any of these scenarios can qualify you to be the recipient of a life's lemon.

What do you do? Actually, what should you not do? First, do not take it personally. Bad things tend to happen in multiples. Lemons rain on the just as well as the unjust. Bad things do happen to good and bad people. It's rough out here. Life is not a picnic.

In Ecclesiastes 3:1–8, the wisest man in the Bible, Solomon, wrote:

> *To everything there is a season, and a time for every matter or purpose under heaven:*
>
> *A time to be born and a time to die, a time to plant and a time to pluck up what is planted,*
> *A time to kill and a time to heal, a time to break down and a time to build up,*

A time to weep and a time to laugh, a time to mourn and a time to dance,
A time to cast away stones and a time to gather stones together, a time to embrace and a time to refrain from embracing,
A time to get and a time to lose, a time to keep and a time to cast away,
A time to rend and a time to sew, a time to keep silence and a time to speak,
A time to love and a time to hate, a time for war and a time for peace.

Lemons are the sour, icky things that just show up sometimes. Whether accidents or purposes, they come and stay awhile. A life lemon can be:

- illness
- domestic violence
- incarceration
- debt
- natural disasters
- your past
- death of someone you love

There are many more of life's lemons, but let's examine each of these lemons a bit closer over the next few chapters. We will ponder ways to react profitably when one comes your way and learn how you can turn life's lemon into lemonade stands.

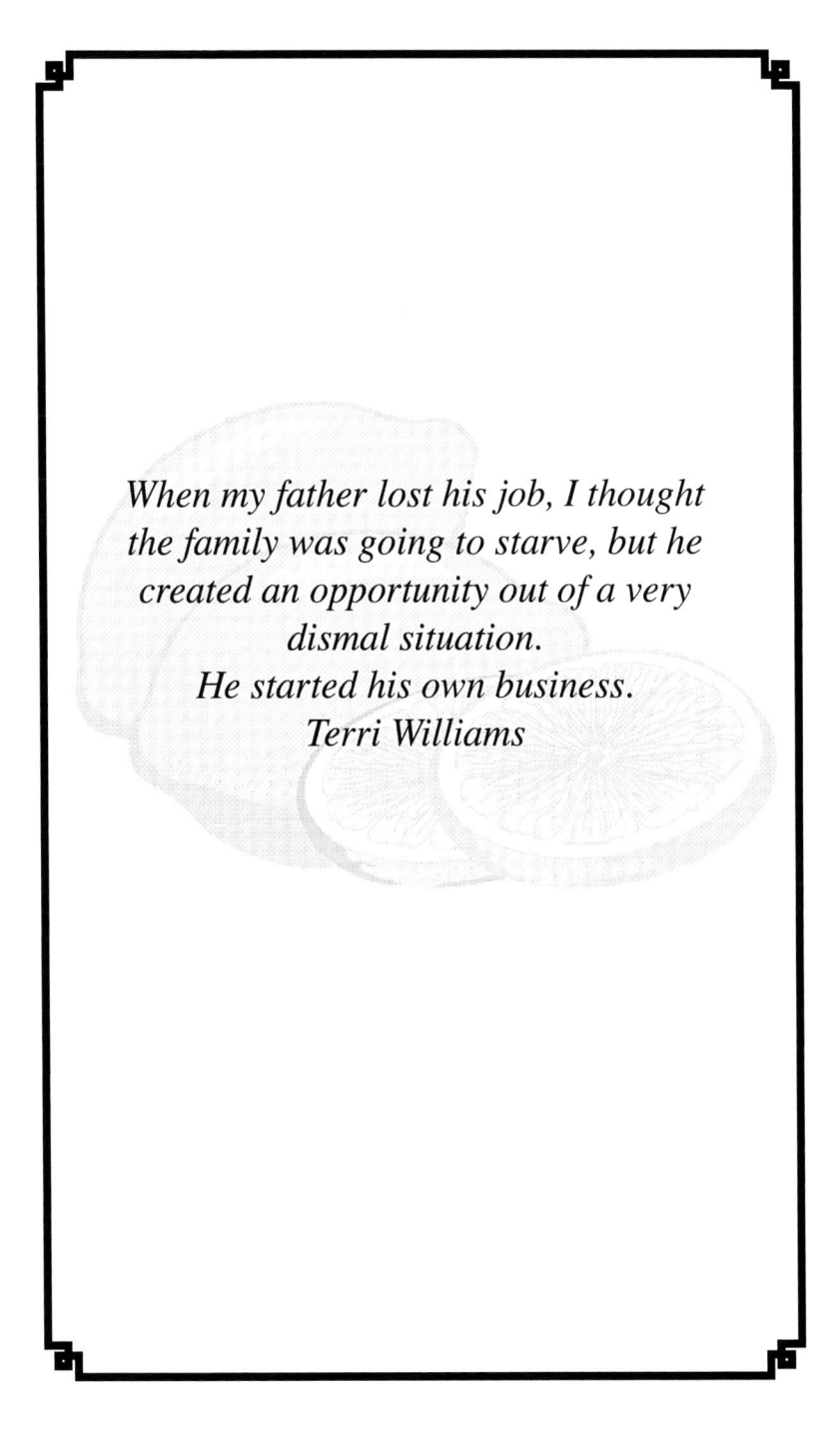

*When my father lost his job, I thought the family was going to starve, but he created an opportunity out of a very dismal situation.
He started his own business.*
Terri Williams

Your Worst Time? Best Time for Business

What do you have to lose? What's left? How much lower can you go? Which way is up? Yes, it is bad. Why now, during one of the worst times in life, should someone even think about starting or developing a business of all things? Some would say that's a preposterous idea.

Preposterous indeed! A small business is an opportunity to create an economic vehicle to start anew. By creating a business, you no longer need to rely on anyone else to give you some of the things you need to make your life better. You can control your own income, time, promotions, and raises. By owning a small business, you quickly learn that it will grow if you work hard and put effort into the business.

Small business owners have personal freedom and a self-sufficient awareness. They are confident that their counterparts in the traditional employment community do not have the same qualities as them. A small business can offer new opportunities for hard-working individuals. Business counselors and training programs can provide access to the assistance, counseling, and confidence that an entrepreneur will need. They can also provide access to business capitalization or savings plans to help achieve success.

The worst time can also be the best time to consider new ways to build assets. For too long, the entire American education system and people in general have been "employment-dependent." Most individuals continuing higher education only want a good job with a good company. Employment is one way to make money, but it is not the only way. Because Americans have focused on building résumés and training for employment, the traditional job with traditional hours has become the gold standard of success. Sadly, not as many community business role models are accessible. Even fewer simple roadmaps lead to business success. When we consider the concept of self-employment, however, the notion of success in business seems attainable. Whether coming from a prison, homeless shelter, bankruptcy, illness, hospital, rehabilitation center, mental institution, place of violence, or natural disaster, someone else has already walked this same road and turned the tables on the unpleasant circumstances to find a more pleasant end. It is possible to build a business during the worst time. When potential and possibility adopt a mind-set that there isn't anything to lose, the creative process begins. A world of profit is available to anyone at any time, even the worst time.

Many individuals have faced these same hindrances and wondered, "What do I do now? Can anything good come from such a bad place?" Believe it or not, the answer is yes!

Why work for the man?
Why not you be the man?

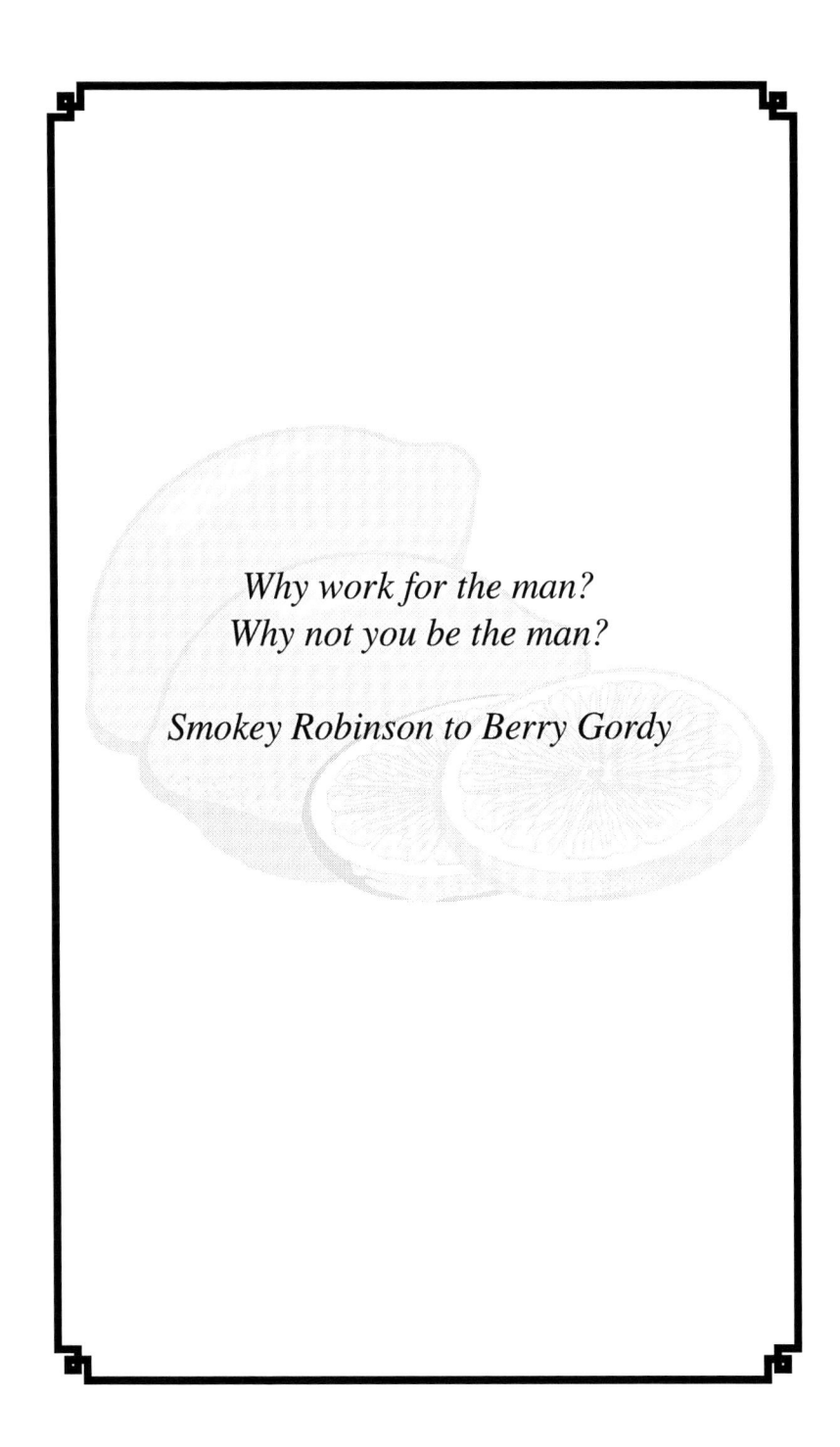

Smokey Robinson to Berry Gordy

Okay, Now What? Take the E Test

Take the Elizabeth Wilson version of the entrepreneurship test! Remember that this is a test of your ability to think and act in an entrepreneurial fashion. For best results, do not try to anticipate the responses or try to come up with the right answer. The first answer that comes to mind is right for you.

The Basics

- Can you spell entrepreneur?
- Have you ever bought or sold anything?
- Do you prefer writing your name on the front of a check to pay for something or writing your name on the back of a check to make a deposit?
- Do you like money? Would you choose to have more or less of it?
- Has anyone ever told you what to do? If so, did you like it?
- Have you ever had a personal hobby? Have you ever seen anyone make money from the same hobby you listed?
- Have you ever done any of the following when you were young: sold candy or food items; delivered newspapers; mowed lawns, baby-sat children; or completed chores in return for an allowance?
- Have you ever recognized a need and filled it?

Business Vision
- Have you ever had a terrific idea for a business?
- Have you ever told anyone about your idea?
- Have you done any of the following about your idea for a business: saved a little money to get started or told everyone you know about your idea?
- If you're thinking of starting a business, which of the following should be your first step: start the business; apply for financing at a bank; or prepare a business plan exploring your concept, strategy, resources and requirements

Character
- Which of the following describes you when you encounter a setback: give up_ fight back_ or solicit others' experience to learn how to get where you want to go?
- If you started your own business, which of the following would describe your family's reaction: think you are joking; provide complete support; or wonder why you can't work for a traditional company?
- Which of the following describes you after hearing criticism: criticize the other person; feel a little bothered; or ignore the criticism completely and decide not to dwell on the negative?

Success
- Which of the following is the most common reason that entrepreneurs give for the success of their businesses: good, well-timed product; personal brilliance, or excellent follow-through?
- Which of the following do entrepreneurs rate as most important to business success: competitiveness; willingness to take initiative; or encouragement?
- Which of the following describes how you best describe business success: gaining wealth, fame, and fortune; business survival, or accomplishing what you attempt?

Marketing
- Which of the following defines marketing: work for Saturdays; a difficult concept for business; or simply selling products or services?

Now, check your score! Wait! Who has time? Let's talk about making money instead!

Lemons

Sour Things

I had to make my own living and my own opportunity. Don't sit down and wait for the opportunities to come; you have to get up and make them.
Madam C.J. Walker

Lemon #1
Illness and Disability

Health issues can be lemons. Talk about feeling squeezed! People with disabilities are considered the largest minority group in America, and, sadly, this group is growing. According to the congressional committee findings for the American Association of Disabled Persons, nearly one out of every five persons is disabled in some manner.[2] Other sources indicate even higher figures. More unfortunate, one-third of disabled Americans are sixty-five or older.[3]

There are hundreds of different kinds of disabilities, including blindness, hearing loss, loss of limbs, and so forth. Some people are born with a disability, but less than 15 percent of individuals are born with their disability. The rest are affected later in life because of illness or accident.

Having a disability during the time of life when you should be most productive is a lemon. Approximately 29.5 million Americans with disabilities are between the employment ages of fifteen to sixty-four. Of these individuals, almost half have a severe disability.[4]

Within the other age groups, 2.9 million children have a disability.[5] The group of individuals who are sixty-five years old and over is the most severely disabled. Of the 16.5 million adults in this age range with a disability, 10.4 million have a severe disability.

Consider the following facts about disability in America: [6]
- For persons without a disability, the employment rate is 80.5 percent. For those with a severe disability that limits their employment opportunities, the employment rate is only 27.6 percent.[7]
- On average, the monthly wage for people between the ages of thirty-five to fifty-four without a disability is $2,446 per month. In comparison, those in the same age range with a non-severe disability have an average monthly earning of $2,006. Those with a severe disability have an average monthly wage of $1,562.[8]
- One million people use wheelchairs.[9]
- Every year, 10,000 people have spinal cord injuries. According to the United States Department of Health, 82 percent of spinal cord injuries happen to males. An estimated 307,000 people younger than forty-four years old use wheelchairs.[10]
- The group of young African-American men using wheelchairs has grown dramatically because they are increasingly the victims of shootings and other violence-related activities.[11]

Communities, employers, service agencies, and families need to be prepared for the tens of thousands of physically injured veterans returning from conflicts in Iraq and Afghanistan. Many returning disabled veterans will find it hard to fit comfortably into traditional employment settings. According to the Insurance Information Institute, from the start of Operation Iraqi Freedom in March 2003 through Jan. 31, 2006, 16,598 military personnel had been physically wounded in action, an average of 474 per month.

Ill health sometimes happens to the best of us. It can happen suddenly in an accident or progressively and gradually. It can happen in the prime of life. Health issues can change your life quickly. The focus on health and health maintenance should take top priority over everything else. Health maintenance can become your most important activity.

Illness lemons include a range of disorders brought on by lifestyle, lack of access to proper health care, or genetics. These diseases include:
- lung disease
- heart disease
- kidney failure
- muscular dystrophy
- multiple sclerosis
- cerebral palsy
- cancer
- controlled diabetes
- arthritis
- asthma
- epilepsy
- HIV/AIDS
- alcoholism
- and former drug use

A Special Note about African Americans with Disabilities
African Americans are more likely than Caucasians to incur many of these debilitating diseases. The overall rate of disability is 20.2 percent for whites, 24.9 percent for African Americans, and 19.2 percent for Hispanics.[12] Approximately 20 million Americans have kidney disease, but this disease is one of the major illnesses to disproportionately impact African Americans.[13] Consider the following information about kidney disease:

- African Americans are nearly four times more likely than Caucasians to develop kidney failure, which requires dialysis or a kidney transplant. African Americans comprise about 12 percent of the population but account for 32 percent of people with kidney failure.[14]
- Among new patients whose kidney failure was caused by high blood pressure, 51.2 percent are African American.[15]
- Among new patients whose kidney failure was caused by diabetes, 31.3 percent are African American.[16]

- African-American men between the ages of twenty and twenty-nine are ten times more likely to develop kidney failure due to high blood pressure than Caucasian men in the same age group. African-American men between the ages of thirty and thirty-nine are about fourteen times more likely to develop kidney failure due to high blood pressure than Caucasian men in the same age group.[17]

Lemonade Success Story: CATHERINE'S STORY

My loving mother, Catherine Agee Williams, was afflicted with the lemons of high blood pressure and strokes, which eventually progressed to renal failure. Over the years, she slowly lost her mobility and agility. After several debilitating strokes, she was unable to continue her work at St. Luke's Hospital in St. Louis, where she had been a central supply worker for many years. This disability took a toll on her body, but her mind, spirit, and tenacity were as strong as ever. Even though her traditional work life was over, she continued to work as the first lady of our church until she was too ill to continue. However, if a person has lost mobility, his or her mind is still not lost.

About a year before her passing, my siblings and I tried to see who could recite the most Bible verses. We did it in a round-robin fashion. All of us, even my heathenish brother Robert, held our own against her for a while. After the third and fourth round, Robert dropped out.

By the fifth or sixth round, my sisters and I had resorted to New Testament scriptures only. As a last resort, we even reached for "Jesus wept". When the last of us had given up, Mama kept going. We begged her to stop, but she would not. She recited verses until we cried "Uncle!" She ruled and reigned from her wheelchair, walker, and cane. She even worked against a body that was determined to fail her. She succeeded in all she tried to accomplish.

With the right type of determination, what is a business plan except a few pieces of paper? One automobile accident or stray bullet can easily take a person from earning wages to being a number on a case management file. A person can instantly become dependent on a monthly disability or social security check for survival. Being a person with a disability or serious illness is a lemon, but you can open a lemonade stand with a disability. Some entrepreneurs with disabilities started or seriously began to develop their businesses after their disability. Why?

- They wanted to add additional income to a disability or social security check.
- They now had more time on their hands to pursue a passion.
- They felt well enough to do something to generate extra income, maybe just not well enough to do what they did before their disability.
- Being productive is enjoyable.
- They wanted to prove the naysayer wrong.
- They didn't need a perfect body to run a great business.
- Technology made it easier to start a business of any type despite a disability.
- The business idea supported others in their situation. They identified an underserved market opportunity.
- They wanted to do it.
- They simply could.

For every dollar spent to rehabilitate disabled persons for traditional employment, at least $10 is returned into our economy.[18] There is ability in every disability. We have all heard the stories of people like Raymond, the Dustin Hoffman character in Rain Man. They may be quite capable or extraordinary in math, music, or the sciences.

Business focuses on abilities and skills. Support programs and national organizations in the United States, such as the Abilities Fund; provide support for business skills development for people with disabilities. Other state agencies, including vocational rehabilitative services, may provide a level of support for adaptive equipment. National microloan programs are also available to help provide access to capital.

A person with a disability can operate quite a few businesses successfully. Examples include writer, artist, Web designer, health care consultant, editor, sports commentator, florist, graphic designer, or service care provider.

Health issues are sometimes invisible. For example, mental illness is a debilitating disease that can impact one's ability to work a traditional job with traditional hours. Employment is only one of the ways to generate income. The fastest-growing group of entrepreneurs in the United States is entrepreneurs with disabilities.

Over the last few years, for people with disabilities, interest has steadily grown in self-employment. This is partially due to research showing that people with disabilities report self-employment at a higher rate than the general population. On average, 20 to 25 percent of people with disabilities are interested in starting businesses.[19] Because of consistently high unemployment rates among people with disabilities, many would apparently choose the option to pursue self-employment if it was made available. Self-employment for people with disabilities is on the rise for the following reasons:

• Self-employment and home-based businesses are a growing trend in America. Telecommunications, the Internet, and outsourcing are contributing factors. People with disabilities now have more economic development options than ever before.

- Self-employment may be the best option available for people with disabilities who live in rural area where employment options are scarce. In order to earn income and support themselves, many people in rural areas have to create a job opportunities for themselves.
- Small businesses are good businesses. Research indicates that 80 percent of small businesses are still operating after eight years. New analysis indicates that previous published figures of failure rates as high as 90 percent were in error. If a business was sold or incorporated or if the owner chose to retire, this business was erringly called a failure.

Most businesses started by people with disabilities meet the definition of a microenterprise, a business with five or fewer employees. It is usually a sole proprietorship with capital needs of less than $35,000 to begin.[20] The rewards of self-employment are more than just generating revenue or acquiring the power to accommodate one's own needs. Intrinsic rewards make the risk and investment in time and money worthwhile. Between 5 and 20 percent of people with disabilities have micro businesses.[21]

In the last five years, several extremely successful entrepreneurs and leaders with some level of disability have credited their business acumen and track records of business achievement to their ability to overcome and compensate for a potentially disabling condition. These successful business leaders learned outside the traditional and mainstream educational lines and transferred those experiences to the business world. A feature article in the May 12, 2002, issue of Fortune showcased these men and women. More recently, the October 2005 cover story for the Atlantic Monthly described the gloom and insight experienced by one of our former presidents, Abraham Lincoln.

Many CEOs and founders of successful companies who had to struggle with disabilities, illnesses, and learning differences have been among the most successful entrepreneurs. The list of successful entrepreneurs with dyslexia include:

- Paul Orfalea (founder of Kinko's)
- Richard Branson (founder and chairman of Virgin group)
- John Chambers (CEO of Cisco Systems)
- Ted Turner (media entrepreneur), Henry Ford (automaker)
- Walt Disney (entertainment entrepre-neur)
- F.W. Woolworth (retailer)
- Alexander G. Bell (telephone inventor)

Other business persons with disabilities include:

- Charles Schwab (founder of Charles Schwab Corporation)
- Diane Swonk (chief economist for Mesirow Financial)
- Tommy Hilfiger (fashion designer)
- Ingvar Kamprad (founder of IKEA)
- David Neeleman (founder and former CEO of JetBlue Airways)
- Raymond Kurzweil (founder of Kurzweil Educational Systems)

Lemonade Success Story:
TANYA'S STORY

Tanya manages a free quarterly magazine for parents of pre-school children. The magazine provides information about child care availability and is financed through advertisements. Tanya also facilitates quarterly workshops for people interested in beginning or developing child care businesses, significantly increasing her income while improving the quality of child care available in her community. Tanya, a quadriplegic, uses a wheelchair, but she also has a can-do, long-term view on life that provides motivation to all around her.

Lemonade Success Story:
SHARON'S STORY

A few years ago, Sharon was homeless and struggling with drug addiction. She and her seven children moved in and out of various transitional homes. Determined to offer her children a brighter future, Sharon decided to turn her life around. She heard about business development classes from her local DFCS. A few months later, she enrolled in a self-employment training research and development class.

A few weeks into the class, Sharon decided she wanted to start and run a transitional home for homeless and abused women. Program staff initially tried to steer Sharon toward a less complex activity, but she was determined to develop her idea. Sharon first identified a house to buy and sponsors who were interested in financing her project. She bought furniture from the local Goodwill store and used DFCS case management services to help her stay on track. She also took advantage of money management and marketing assistance classes. Four homeless women eventually moved into the house. One year later, her transitional home was always filled to capacity with six residents. The local housing authority and other social service agencies provided funding.

Sharon and her seven children now live in their own home. Her children are proud of their mother. They are proud to be able to help with her successful venture. Sharon is now opening her second transitional home to house thirteen more women who are struggling with the same issues she faced in her life. Sharon has truly succeeded against the odds!

Lemonade Success Story:
BIG COOL

Big Cool was a young African American man with a winning personality. He had high blood pressure, which led to severe diabetes. He lost a leg to the illness, so he used a wheelchair for mobility.

Big Cool loved music, so he decided to supplement his income by burning music to mixed CDs. Over a short period of time, his customer base grew as did his skills in marketing and packaging the best tunes. If Big Cool didn't have the music you wanted, he'd get it. He focused his energy on customer service. He knew the types of music that his customers wanted before they did. His office was located in the business center of the Goodwill store. Until he passed, he would set up shop and then make and his sell his products. To this day, whenever I want to hear some truly mellow music, I just go to my Big Cool collection and pop in a CD.

Persons with disabilities can access several resources to find out more about business opportunities. One of the best national organizations in the country that provides entrepreneurial training services, resources, and funding for people with disabilities is the Abilities Fund (www.abilitiesfund.org). It provides training and works with vocational rehabilitation agencies across the country to raise awareness about entrepreneurship.

Vocational rehabilitation services can also provide a level of financial support to individuals whose business ideas are taken through a vetting process by a self-employment program or counselor. I have worked with vocational rehabilitation to assess client business ideas. In turn, vocational rehabilitation approved the purchase of adaptive equipment, such as computers and software, and other materials to help businesses grow and prosper.

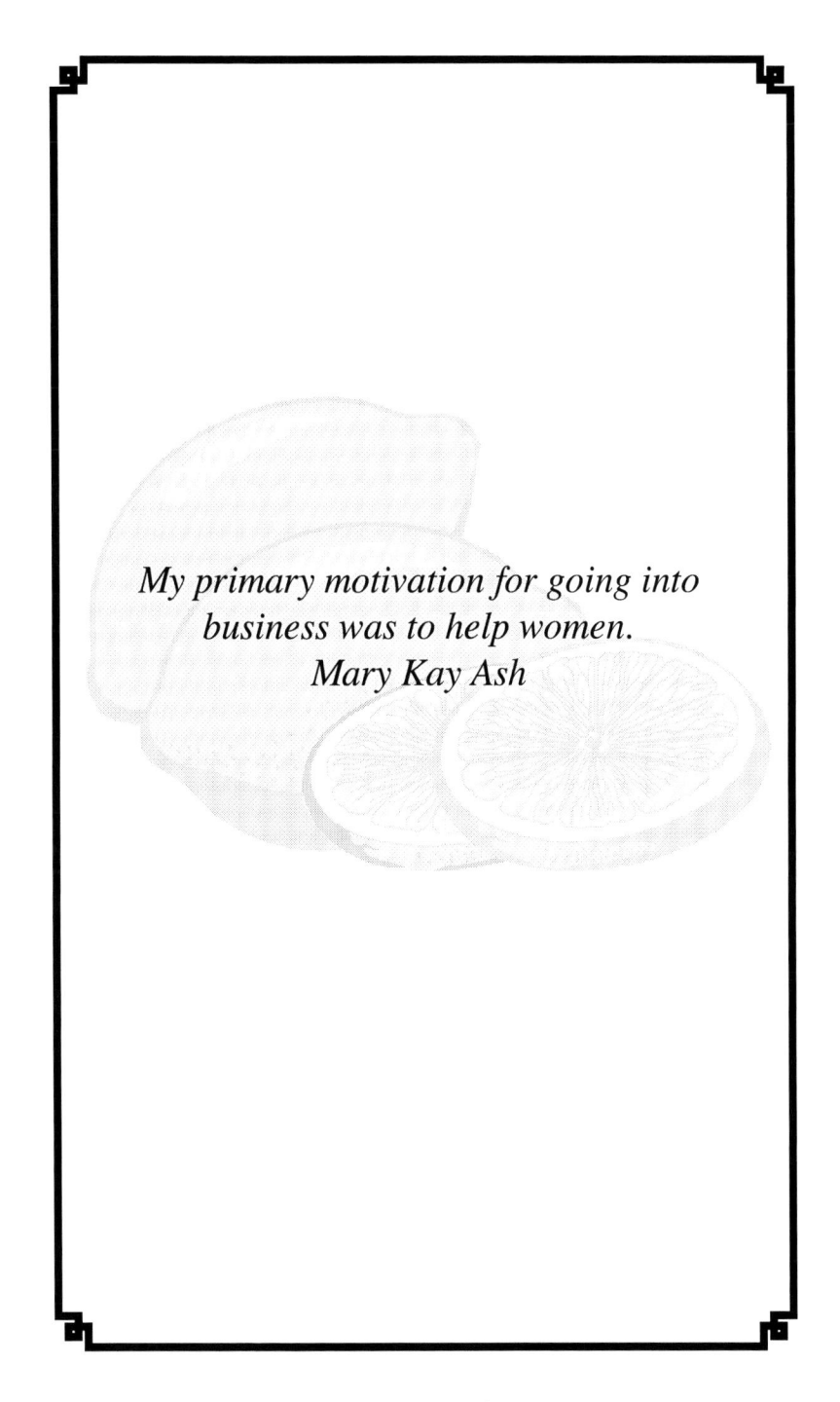

My primary motivation for going into business was to help women.
Mary Kay Ash

Lemon #2
Domestic Violence

Domestic violence is a lemon. Having a loved one suffer physical or mental harm is devastating. Recent startling statistics reveal that one out of every four women is a victim of domestic violence.[22] When a woman is in a domestic violence situation, her first thought is for safety and survival. She must flee to survive. Many times, survivors go to shelters because family and friends may refuse to harbor them again. Others may think, "Not this time." The victim goes to a shelter because she fears that her attacker may know where she and other family members live and may come after her as well as well as her loved ones.

Survivors note that their lack of money is the primary deterrent to leaving an abusive and dangerous relationship. According to a national poll on domestic violence that the National Network to End Domestic Violence and AllState Foundation conducted, 60 percent of survivors surveyed said a lack of financial resources is one of the main challenges to leaving an abusive situation. Other findings from the study included:

- 30 percent said money is the single biggest obstacle to escape, second only to fear of the abuser finding them.
- 75 percent said emergency funds would be helpful.

- 66 percent said victims could benefit from job training.
- More than 50 percent said financial training would be useful.
- 75 percent said they know someone who has been a victim of domestic violence.
- More than 80 percent said the problem equally impacts people of all races, educational levels, and socioeconomic backgrounds.[23]

Special Note on Women as Survivors of Domestic Violence
There are 6.4 million women-owned businesses in the United States, the fastest-growing segment of business owners.[24] Sales receipts for female-owned businesses have more than doubled since 1987.[25] Women of all types and from all walks of life own their own businesses.

Many women start businesses during the rough times of their lives. Business development is a source of additional revenue and comfort. The growing segments of women who are creating businesses by any means necessary include women in the following categories:

- **Public assistance recipients**: Women who receive public assistance, such as Temporary Assistance to Needy Families (TANF) or food stamps, are sometimes motivated to work their way out of poverty through self-employment rather than working for others. According to statistics from DFCS, 2 to 5 percent of women seeking to end dependence on TANF seek self-employment. [26]

- **Women caring for families:** Women choose self-employment in order to have more flexible schedules or work from home so they can care for young children, disabled family members, or aging parents.

- **Women with disabilities:** Women with disabilities who have been dependent on public assistance often engage in self-employment to help become more independent in ways that accommodate their disabilities and fulfill entrepreneurial desires.

- **Female immigrants and refugees:** Women who immigrate to the United States to escape political persecution or domestic violence situations or find new economic opportunities frequently start businesses to help support themselves and their families. Many cultures set a high value on entrepreneurial activities and embrace the American dream of owning a small business. Maybe that's why the Statue of Liberty is a woman. She is a symbol of safety and security in another land.

- **Women who are recently or frequently unemployed:** Women dislocated from their jobs for various reasons turn to self-employment,[27] especially in the current environment of high unemployment. Two to five percent of people seeking unemployment insurance seek self-employment. Also, the frequently unemployed, women who get fired, or women who get tired quite often tend to gravitate toward self-employment and find freedom when they can work on their own and be their own bosses.

- **Working poor women:** Women working in low-wage, part-time, or unreliable jobs will sometimes turn to self-employment to supplement their income or try to create a more stable source of income for themselves and their families.

- **Women in transition:** Women in a transitional situation frequently engage in short-term, odd jobs to meet basic needs. Self-employment offers opportunities to use one's talents and find personal fulfillment.

- **Glass ceiling women:** Women who have reached the apex of their careers with nowhere else to go realize they can do for themselves what they have done for someone else. It's no fun walking around with your back bowed because you are bent over from the ceiling of being underemployed. Because of the traditional barriers to job advancement, many women find that they cannot advance on their jobs, no matter what they do. No manner of talent, skill, or motivation will break through the glass ceiling.

These multiple motivations for business ownership are driving the dramatic growth in female-owned businesses in the United States. Some of these same motivations will drive domestic violence survivors who want financial security for themselves and their children. Domestic violence survivors who must leave their employment to avoid encountering their abusers have additional motivation to find a source of income that might be less public or allow them more flexibility during their transitional situation.

Small or micro businesses that receive support from micro-enterprise development training programs demonstrate tenacity with survival rates of 57 to 90 percent.[28] Survival rates compare very favorably to the general population of small businesses. The United States Small Business Administration estimates that only 47 percent of small businesses are still operating after four years.[29] These businesses grow and become profitable, contributing to increases in personal and household income. This percentage is higher and more favorable than generally noted for start-up businesses.

Although many business owners patch their income together from several sources, studies indicate that small businesses who receive supportive business training services can become major contributors to increased household income.[30]

Unless cornered, women generally tend to think too small. For women to be able to think big enough, they sometimes need pressure. For example, consider the story of the mother who saw her child pinned under a car and produced the strength to move the vehicle and free the child from harm. Under normal circumstances, without being squeezed, she would not be able to realize her potential power. Without pressure, she would never have fathomed actually succeeding at an impossible task.

The benefits of self-employment cannot be defined in purely financial terms. The non-financial benefits are especially important for domestic violence survivors. Operating a business generates a host of other benefits for its owner, family, and community. The business owner gains a level of control over her life, even though she might work very long hours. When asked about the benefits of operating a business, many business owners speak of fulfilling a dream, feeling proud of a well-done job, gaining a sense of security, finding support networks, and increasing self-esteem that reverberates throughout other parts of their lives. New skills, managerial capacity, and attitudes develop that strengthen a survivor's capacity to run a business and their lives. The non-financial benefits can be almost as valuable, if not more, than the actual income generated.

The self-confidence, sense of security, and other non-financial benefits are very important to women who had their sense of self-worth undermined and their sense of security attacked. Businesses, especially micro businesses, can start on almost nothing. Let's think of a domestic violence situation in terms of a race.

- **Ready:** In the midst of a domestic violence situation, a survivor can use the thought of a business to help see other life possibilities. If a person cannot safely attend a business planning class, they can still read stories of successful entrepreneurs such as Madam C. J. Walker, a victim of domestic violence and the first African American millionaire in America. One thought strategy is to begin to channel the lives of these great entrepreneurs. A survivor can meditate and pray for direction and guidance about ways to keep her home and self safe and calm. This is a time of calm and thought. In her autobiography, Tina Turner shared her story of abuse and how she got ready to escape. In the movie, she depicted a scene after a horrendous fight with her then-husband, Ike Turner. She did not leave Ike after that fight. Rather, she left much later when he was sleeping and she had a chance to prepare herself and her mind to go. She prayed and meditated to help her obtain the internal fortitude she needed to move her life forward. Knowing when it is safe to steal away is the time to get ready. A survivor can use wisdom to prepare mentally first. Visioning is free. If you will allow it to work for you, you can tap into a hidden, but internal, source of unstoppable power. This power is available to all. You can harness it to do great things. This power is unlimited and abundant. There is no lack in it. Honor the strength of others who have come or gone before you. Learn from their paths and lives. Learn from their mistakes and envision yourself in their stories. Read your name into their lives. Respect, reflect, and get ready.

- **Set:** This is the time to prepare yourself and develop your skill. Hone your craft at home, out of public view. Work on your hobby whenever your can. If you can do something to improve it, do it. Can you add perfection to your skill? Do it. Can you take it to the next level? Do it. Are you working in that field? Do it. Can you do it without tipping off the abuser, making him angry and creating disharmony in your home? Do it. Can you do it without triggering his anger? Do it. Can you do it without taking time away from your children? Do it. What others things are you doing that are expendable right now? What can you give up so you can have more time to work on your special talent? Do it. Consider this period of your life as a type of diet. It's not forever, but it will help you move toward a goal of independence and self-sufficiency. This can be the planning stage. You can write goals, keep a journal, ask someone to review your plan, take some online business training courses, or contact a business training program. You can research the business or industry you find interesting. You can contact businesses that are similar to the one you are interested in developing. You can think about money and set realistic, SMART goals. Making this time important can help you in many ways. It can be a time for a positive distraction in your life.

- **Go:** This is where many survivors cross over to another life, for example, a women's shelter. A shelter is part of the system of social services. The staff and case managers are most concerned with your immediate needs of safety, shelter, and self-esteem. They may help with the court system, taking your batterer to jail or pressing charges. Another group may help you heal physically, making sure you are taking proper medications and receiving adequate mental health support. You will also encounter other women who will be there to commensurate with you and help you live through this nightmarish period of your life. Eventually, an assigned case worker or case manager will help you navigate your way back to some type of employment or provide you with vouchers, food stamps, tokens, or some level of counseling to meet your immediate needs. A mental health worker may help with issues involving your self-esteem. He or she can talk with you about some of the horrors you have faced. All of these trained professionals are prepared to help you move through the domestic violence system. All of these caregivers are wonderful, needed, and required supports to help you gain enough strength to not go back to the abuser. However, they will not encourage you to pursue self-employment. They will give you the following "not now" reasons for not pursuing self-employment:

- Not now while you are so fragile
- Not now while you are in a shelter
- Not now while you are someone's prey
- Not now while you have a bull's-eye on your back
- Not now while you are using an assumed name
- Not now while out don't have anything left because all of

your clothes are at the house and you only came out with what you had on
- Not now while your kids are crying for their daddy because they didn't see him crack you in the head or, if they did, they still love him because he's their father
- Not now while you can't use your ATM card because you're broke
- Not now while you still have a sore life, black eye, or broken wrist
- Not now while you're still in pain
- Not now while you still in love with him because he did promise to never hit you again.

All of these reasons are lemons. Why not now? Staff of microenterprise development programs have not been trained in domestic violence issues despite the fact that many of the women they serve have faced—or are facing—domestic violence. Many domestic violence survivors can earn income and achieve economic independence through business ownership, but domestic violence programs are not aware of services available to aid them along that path. Providing more effective resources for women who experience domestic violence to pursue entrepreneurship. A shelter though a haven for safety can also feel like a prison: you pass go and get out of a bad relationship and end up in another strange place. You have very little control now. Everybody is taking care of you. For the moment, you are safe. Are you safe enough to dream? Are you safe enough to think about how you came this far by faith? Any prison, shelter, or hellhole is a place to stop, pause, and plan. Liken yourself to Harriett Tubman. She was a slave in the master's house. Still, she knew there was a better place, a place better than her present circumstances.

> ## *Lemonade Success Story:*
> ## CELIE'S STORY
>
> In *The Color Purple* by Alice Walker, Mister beat Celie down so low that she couldn't even hold up her head. But she did have skills. She kept the house, cooked, cleaned, and sewed her stepchildren's clothes. She perfected her skills so well that, even when Mister brought his mistress, Shug Avery, to the house, he kept Celie around. Skills matter. Celie had multiple skills she could have developed and turned into a business. She chose sewing and became a seamstress. She opened a small enterprise called "Miss Celie's Pants." As soon as she had a chance to run away with Shug Avery, she left Mister a good old curse as a parting gift.
>
> Celie thrived by taking the skill she had developed during her lemon days and turned it into a business. With a small bit of capital from an inheritance, she bought some colorful material and began making fancy, comfortable, or colorful pants that women wanted to wear. Before long, all the women in town were wearing Miss Celie's pants. She took the bitterness of domestic violence and hate (lemon), added her natural skills (water), and turned it into something sweet and profitable, Miss Celie's pants (a lemonade stand). She began thriving as a self-sufficient entrepreneur. She turned her focus to herself and her business. She became a fruitful woman again.

A transitional shelter is a temporary home. When you arrive, you are given the title of domestic violence survivor. Like a breast cancer or holocaust survivor, you are out. You have survived. It probably doesn't feel like that, though. Even after a tooth is removed, a limb is severed, or a breast is taken, the pain is still there. But the thing that caused the pain is now gone. Now, you have the lemon, the scar or broken life, to prove it. But your status is deemed as survivor.

Being a domestic violence survivor pushes you to another level. If you survived him and the things that happened between you, you can survive other things as well. Many times, shelter workers are also domestic violence survivors. Their misery is their ministry. What doesn't kill you makes you stronger. You've been through the worst. Many would-be entrepreneurs have never faced rejection, risk, pain, lack, doing without, or losing it all. Does any of that sound familiar to you? People around you want to insulate you from further pain and suffering. You have been to hell and back. What is a business plan to you? What stress would a business training class cause you to have? Financial statement? Bring it on!

Business development is a distraction, but it can be managed on the run. The tools are mainly internal. People don't carry their inventory with them anymore. You can start where you are with what you have. If you have skills, you can take them with you. You are your business. If you have lost your self-esteem, one of the best ways to get it back is to make your own money. I disagree with the common thinking that the atmosphere must be perfect for business development. Opportunities abound. Markets are everywhere. New products and services are revealed every day.

During your shelter stage, it will be very difficult to get any approvals, buy-ins, support, or financial access for a business. If you can find some type of employment, your support system will want you to concentrate on acquiring a job and learning the required skills. Your family will want you to concentrate on safety first. They would not endorse that you take on anything that might put you at risk.

You will have a hard time finding any traditional business support services now. Most micro- or small business training curriculum are created for people who work and have an address, social security number, contact information, verifiable income, and so forth. Micro enterprise development organizations are also very systemic. They expect you to have a name, not an alias, if they are going to train you for a start-up business. They don't know you or know you are on the run for whatever reason. Classes meet after traditional business hours, on weekends, or during evening hours. At these times, shelters expect you to be locked inside. Your abuser may be around after working hours. There has been little dialogue or resources to date between the domestic violence and MED community. MED programs lean toward the development of legitimate functional businesses, that is, ones that are stable and trackable. Social security numbers and family contact information are all required.

Being anonymous is usually not an option. You receive services in exchange for detailed personal information. But no one can keep you from participating in self-paced, business training classes if you choose to do so.

You may have to facilitate the initial dialogue between your case worker and business development trainers. This is when your preparation will work for you. Show you have thought your business idea through. Show you are prepared to work together with both the domestic violence community and small business development community. Having a written business journal or the beginnings of a business plan will also be impressive. The majority of people who attend business training programs have not completed this type of work beforehand.

Getting a buy-in from both parties in advance will be important. Both can work together to provide the support you need in their areas of expertise. You may want to ask if you can audit a business training class first and not feel the pressure to meet all the attendance requirements right away. Ask if you can just sit in when you can. You may forgo graduation requirements and the completion certificate, but you will acquire the business knowledge and skills. Importantly, you will begin to develop the business support networks that will help you work your plan.

Some businesses that domestic violence survivors may want to consider pursing are:
- hairdresser
- artisan
- seamstress
- writer/author/editor
- motivational speaker
- janitor
- caterer
- specialty candy maker
- nail technician
- quilt maker
- card maker
- jewelry maker
- plant/pet keeper
- handyperson
- car detailer
- photographer.

There are some resources for domestic violence survivors to use to help make the case for entrepreneurship. National organizations, like the state domestic violence coalitions, can identify local domestic violence programs in your area. State coalitions are listed on the National Coalition Against Domestic Violence (NCADV) Web site (www.ncadv.org). The NCADV has a personal financial education curriculum entitled "Hope and Power." The manuals are available in both English and Spanish. They are geared toward women who are domestic violence survivors. Free copies of this manual are also available through the NCADV Web site.

Lemonade Success Story:
SHARON'S STORY

Sharon is a cosmetologist who braids hair. She had to flee her home in Chicago with her children after repeated instances of domestic violence from her husband. Even with the order of protection against him, she felt unsafe and feared he would find her. She finally landed at a women's shelter in Atlanta. When she arrived at her first business training class, she used an assumed name and felt uncomfortable providing information to the program about her previous address. While staying at a women's shelter, her case worker encouraged her to pursue her previous occupation. Her case worker helped her identify a local small business training program in the area. She came to a local MED program to fund her supplies and provide marketing materials to reestablish her business in Atlanta. In addition to a small microloan, she found support and encouragement from the other women in her class.

If you do right, right will follow you.
Oprah Winfrey

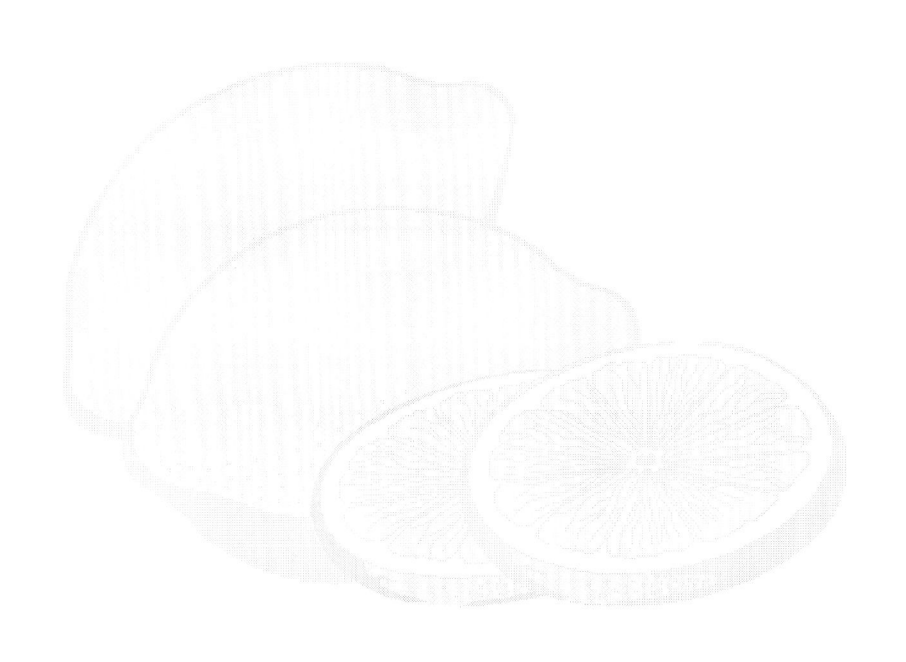

Lemon # 3
Incarceration

Incarceration is a lemon that impacts the economy, families, communities, and individuals. In 2003, Devah Pager, a sociologist, found that a criminal record is associated with a 50 percent reduction in employment opportunities for whites and a 64 percent reduction for African Americans. More than two million individuals are incarcerated in prisons and jails in the United States.[31] Other sobering statistics about incarceration include:

- More than 650,000 prisoners are released from prison each year. Ten million will cycle in and out of local jails.
- More than 67 percent will be arrested again. Fifty percent will return to prison.
- More than 25 percent of the population has been arrested.
- An estimated 4.6 million individuals are on probation.
- Seven million individuals have churned through our jail system.
- One out of thirty-seven people have served extensive time.
- One-third of African American men will be arrested.
- One out of nineteen African American women will be arrested.
- One-fourth of all arrests are women.
- One-third of released individuals will end up back in prison

or jail within three years of returning to their community.
- Eighty percent of ex-offenders return to prison after five years.
- More than two million juveniles under the age of twenty-four are in the adult prison system.[32]

In 2006, the Bureau of Justice Statistics reported expenditures on state corrections departments rose from $6 billion in 1982 to $39 billion in 2003, an increase of 550 percent.[33]

Over the past few years, opportunities for incarcerated individuals to participate in vocational training programs while in prison have decreased significantly. It is estimated that less than 27 percent of incarcerated individuals participate in vocational training programs.[34] But many people use their lockdown time to pursue education programs to further their education. Incarcerated youth are required to attend educational programs until they are sixteen years old. While incarcerated, some individuals have completed their GED programs. A few have even attained law degrees. Depending on the length of the sentence and available resources in the prison, an incarcerated individual can make good educational use of his time away.

I believe entrepreneurship can be taught. While a person is serving time, he or she should make it work on his or her behalf. Many inmates spend time honing their bodies to become fine-tuned machines. In the end, when an offender leaves prison, what does he or she leave with in the long run? Sadly, even when an offender leaves prison with an education, he or she is now considered to be an educated ex-offender.

Employment applications are required for most traditional employment opportunities. If you check "yes" on the employment form, you can say good-bye to the job. Many times, an ex-offender will not be hired for the job, possibly not even considered. The typical human resource personnel or job interviewer does not even care about the education you acquired in lockdown. Many ex-offenders speak eloquently and think brilliantly because they have honed their mental capacities reading, writing, and planning. However, the recidivism rate is startling.

In general, people either fear, hate, or feel ashamed of ex-offenders. Across the country, single women blame the high incarcerations rates on the low numbers of potential marriage partners. Federal and state laws bar or restrict ex-offenders from holding certain licenses and certifications. Ex-offenders are restricted to participate in only certain networking opportunities. These restrictions severely limit an ex-offender's participation in occupations such as health care, child care, transportation, and security.

What would happen if offenders were permitted to access materials to develop small businesses and business plans while in prison? Many incarcerated persons spend hours writing love letters to girlfriends or potential girlfriends. Could they channel that same energy into developing a thoughtful business plan? Incarcerated individuals spend hours writing to loved ones, or potential loved ones, while incarcerated. Could they channel that pent-up need into writing a business concept paper or doing some research and development on a potential enterprise? To start a business plan, an individual only needs a piece of paper, a pen, and access to business training materials. If none of these items are available, creativity will work.

Though most prisons do not allow incarcerated individuals to access the Internet, most have libraries. Entrepreneurship, business, and industry trade manuals may be available and accessible by request. While in prison, an individual can research possible business enterprises and create a solid, functioning business plan. After being released or put on probation, the individual can pursue these dreams.

I recently facilitated a roundtable of young men who were pursuing entrepreneurship through a business training program. Each one had been incarcerated at some time in his life. All felt their best bets for economic self-sufficiency would be the pursuit of self-employment. All expressed remorse for their past activities and felt they could give back to the community through various business enterprises. They detailed some of the issues that inmates may face after they return to society following extended periods of incarceration:

- **Loss of paper:** Identification (social security cards, driver's licenses, and proper identification) was significant hindrance to reestablishing a place in society.
- **Lack of capital:** When prisoners are discharged, they are given a nominal amount of cash, usually $25 and maybe a bus ticket. Those aren't exactly the tools needed to reestablish credibility.
- **Lack of family support:** Each of the young men expressed sadness that family members were not encouraging their self-employment pursuits. One man even noted that his grandmother was leery. If your grandmother isn't in your corner, what chance do you have?
- **Lack of support** from parole officers and case managers: Ex-offenders are required to pay for many of the services they receive from the parole office. The need for immediate employment opportunities to make money to pay for these services is required.
- **Continuous repayment of the debt to society**: Upon completion of the formal sentence, the informal sentencing continues. The need to repay society is very strong for many ex-offenders. They desire to do well and make up for their previous deed, for example, starting nonprofit organizations, becoming ministers, and so forth. These are great endeavors, but I think that one of the best things a person can do to give back is to be on purpose and profitable. Giving back is great.

Making profit, employing others, and creating viable businesses that help build communities is even better. A concentration on giving back sometimes negates the potential of moving forward and looking beyond to a new future.

Though all of these issues were expressed, each of the young men still felt their chances would be better if they pursued the self-employment route. The pride they felt in their individual enterprises was amazing. The creative energy they had harnessed to move their lives forward was impressive. Even if they only made enough money to employ themselves, staying out of trouble and the penal system is worth the investment of helping these young men all by itself.

A large percentage of inmates come to prison as seasoned entrepreneurs, having run highly successful enterprises like drug rings and gangs. They know how to manage others to get things done. They are passionate, intelligent, and willing to take risks. Even the most unsophisticated drug dealers inherently understand business concepts like competition, profitability, risk management, and the development of proprietary sales channels. What if these influential leaders ran legitimate companies? Though ex-offenders are sometimes limited in the types of licenses and businesses they can start, there are still many businesses to consider.

Lemonade Success Story:
FELONY FRANKS HOT DOG

Chicago entrepreneur Jim Andrews' five employees have all been to prison, and he says they're great employees. Former felons can seldom find work.

"Once they're branded as ex-offender, you might as well just tattoo 'felon' on their foreheads," Jim said.

Enter the idea of Felony Frank's Hot Dogs. Andrews will finance and license hot dog stores to former felons, turning ex-offenders into entrepreneurs through a foundation he set up three years ago. At the Michael Barlow Center, where formerly incarcerated men and women learn job skills to cope in the real world, Bob Dougherty knows giving them a job is important.

"(It's) the component that really signs the deal as to whether or not they will remain on the positive side of the law," Dougherty said.

That's exactly what Jim Andrews hopes to accomplish with the idea of his Felony Franks. Non-offenders need not apply.
"It is felons only," he said.

In addition to hotdog stands, a few small businesses that are easy to start include barber, landscaper, baker/chef, artist/muralist, painter, bricklayer, T-shirt vendor, medical coder, mechanic, personal trainer, handyman, janitor, records researcher, truck driver, car detailer, DJ, vending machine owner, upholsterer, real estate investor, or security consultant.

Prison time is hard time, but it can also be productive time. One of the major requirements of running a business is doing market analysis or industry research. Many people open businesses without having a skill or mastery in that area. When you work for yourself, you don't have to worry about unemployment applications. Unlike other employers, you do hire ex-offenders. You hire yourself!

In some industries, having a prison record is almost a requirement for success. The list of entertainers, rappers, sports figures, and business leaders who have been incarcerated is growing daily, including:

- Martha Stewart (media mogul)
- 50 Cent (rapper)
- Ivan Boesky (Wall Street mogul)
- Leona Helmsley (hotel owner)
- Ping Fu (software firm owner)
- Snoop Dogg (rapper)
- Lil' Kim (rapper)
- James Brown (entertainer)
- Charles Dutton (actor)
- Greg Mathis (television judge)
- Bobby Seale (barbeque sauce entrepreneur)
- Shyne (rapper)
- Flesh-n-Bone (rapper)
- Marion Barry (former mayor/consultant)
- Donny Johnson (artist)
- Michael B. Jackson (writer)
- Carl Rupp (snow cone entrepreneur)
- DMX (rapper)
- David Lewis (motivational speaker)
- Snoop Pearson (actress)
- Kenneth Rushing (real estate investor)
- Paris Hilton (actress/singer)

Lemonade Success Story:
JAMAL'S STORY

Jamal was seventeen when he murdered someone during a robbery. Because of his age, he received a six-year sentence with six to serve. While in prison, Jamal enrolled in the prison GED program and earned his graduation equivalency. Because he had the time, he continued to pursue an education and received his bachelor's degree.

Upon his release from prison, he found employment with a company that hired ex-offenders. His first job was mailroom attendant. Because he knew he had the mental capacity to improve his life, he began to study business manuals and computers. He took information technology classes in the evenings and moved from the mailroom to become a junior programmer at the company. Because of his previous incarceration, he knew he could only go so far in the company. He felt he could do better with his skills on his own and decided to start an IT consulting business.

Jamal felt the stigma of his previous incarceration would always follow him in the company, so he branched out on his own. Because of his skill and knowledge of business, he could acquire several consulting contracts. Within a few years, he advanced his consulting fee to $65 per hour. Jamal now has a six-figure salary as an independent contractor. He hired himself and now feels he has paid back a small portion of his debt to society and his family. Jamal has never returned to a life of crime and enjoys a comfortable, middle-class lifestyle.

Lemonade Success Story:
GINA'S STORY

Gina had several brushes with the law. When she came to a small business training program for a community orientation she announced, "I make the best sweet potato pie in the country!" The following week, she brought samples of her pies to the intake interview. During the interview, she shared her history of incarceration. This was after I tasted her pie. Her incarceration story paled in comparison to the delicious dessert creation. In retrospect, being an ex-offender who happened to be an excellent cook seemed a minor issue. She attended the training classes and provided catering services for many of the organization's events. Gina continued to struggle finding full-time employment, but she always has her cooking skills when she needed money. Through these skills, she worked her way into television appearances and other media opportunities. She has expanded her business to now include motivational speaking and cooking. Gina knew her life was filled with lemons, but she just chopped them up and used them in one of her many delicious recipes.

Few formal resources are available for ex-offenders to find out more about self-employment opportunities. I am working with several national organizations to consider national initiatives to support prisoner reentry through entrepreneurship. One of the most promising has been a dialogue between the criminal justice community and the microenterprise development community supported by the Marion Ewing Kauffman Foundation in Kansas City, Missouri. They have sponsored two conversations on this issue: "Entrepreneurship and Prisoner Reentry: The Concept, the Nuts and Bolts, the Pitch" and "Entrepreneurship and Prisoner Reentry: Ready, Set, Go." I was pleased to be invited to attend the second conversation held in San Diego in December 2006. The outcome of both of these conversations and ongoing dialogue will hopefully create more opportunities for ex-offenders to receive support and encouragement to pursue self-employment training while incarcerated and when they come home to communities across the country. More information about this initiative can be found at www.reentry.gov.

Until then, you have my permission to pursue your self-employment dreams. The world of entrepreneurship does not ask where you've been. Rather, the main question is why has it taken you so long? Ex-offender entrepreneurship reminds me of a segment from the Twilight Zone. A woman found herself despised and hated on her home planet. Everyone who saw her was afraid of her ugliness. The children and women ran when they saw her face. No matter how much plastic surgery she had, in the eyes of her native people, she was to be shunned and feared. The final solution devised was to send her to a different planet with people of her kind who looked like her and accepted her with open arms. The people of her planet viewed her beauty as heinous, but they actually had hideous, monstrous faces. The faces of the people on the new planet were similar to her own, beautiful and accepting.

To entrepreneurial ex-offenders who can find no love in the employment community and are viewed as heinous and feared, come to the world of entrepreneurship. Bring your entrepreneurial skills and talents to a planet of people of your kind, that is, other entrepreneurs. You are welcome here!

*Entrepreneurship is the ultimate
smart money move.
Kelvin Boston*

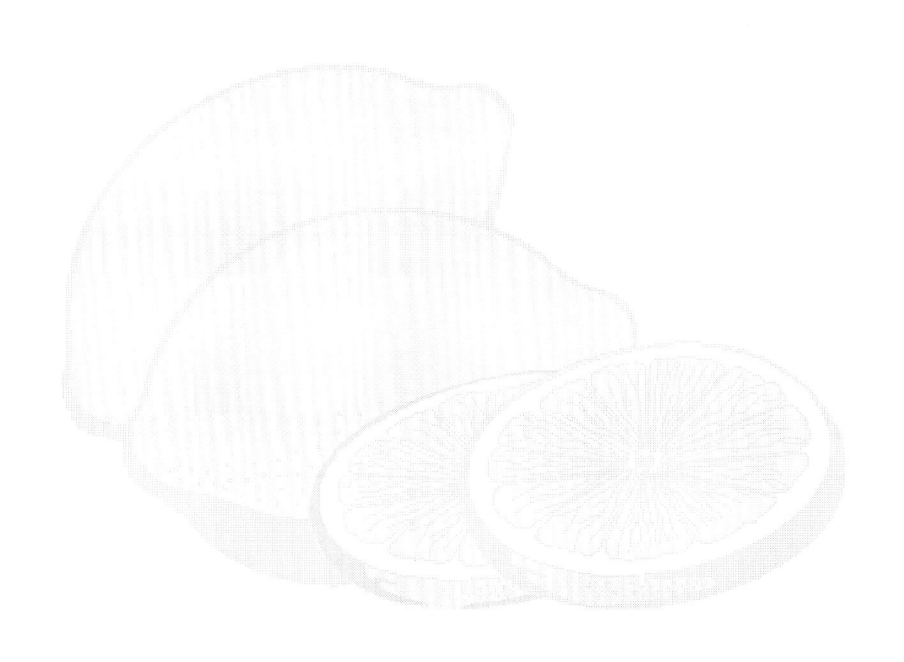

Lemon # 4
Debt

Debt, bankruptcy, student loans, foreclosures, repossessions, and evictions. Do any of these words sound familiar? Bad debt is a sour lemon. Being unable to repay debt is a financial paralysis that takes many people a lifetime to overcome. Some never do. Debt even follows you beyond the grave. Sadly, after you're gone, your survivors will receive calls from your creditors, asking them to pay your debts. They are required to provide a copy of your death certificate to the creditor to stop the harassing calls.

An outstanding student loan or IRS judgments never disappears. A chapter 14 bankruptcy will show up on a credit report for ten years. A chapter 7 bankruptcy remains on a credit report for seven years from the date of discharge. Debt is a big, fat, sour lemon. It will cost you in almost every aspect of your life. Not only does it impact your ability to access additional credit, it also makes you pay more for every other transaction you make. Every time you pay a house or car note, you will pay more than the person with average or pristine credit. A credit score of 600 or less will land you in the bad debt category.

When your credit is bad, you are unable to purchase assets like a home or a business. Some people have been unable to purchase a home for thirty years because of an outstanding student loan. The IRS is unrelenting in its collections process. An IRS judgment refuses to go away and keeps coming back, pursuing you at every turn.

The average age of a person starting a new business in American is thirty-five. For many, a small business is a second, more enjoyable career. It is a means to a new end. But, by the time many people consider developing this business at the age of thirty-five,[35] they have already incurred a significant level of debt, including student loans, additional mortgages, taxes, divorce settlements, judgments, and so forth. Monies are already budgeted and allocated to pay life necessities like utilities, credit cards, food, shelter, and clothing. Finding unallocated money for a business would be, to say the least, very difficult.

That's the bad news for young people in debt. For seniors and the elderly, it only gets worse. A study by Putnam Investments surveyed 2,000 people who had retired at the age of sixty-five within the past two to six years. Their average household income was $49,000. Of the retirees' income, 24 percent came from traditional pensions. Eleven percent came from self-directed accounts and other investments. Forty-one percent came from social security payments. Half of the respondents stated they were living better than in their working years. The other half stated that their quality of life had dropped. Approximately 20 percent reported they were struggling. More than 78 percent regretted not saving more during their work years. Fifty-nine percent felt they should have started saving for retirement earlier in their careers. More than a third wished their employer or plan manager had encouraged them to save more aggressively. Only 16 percent of those surveyed reported they had a formal, written financial plan.[36]

In the December 2004 issue of Money, it was reported that sixty-two percent of Americans reported they were saving and/or investing some money. However, more than 40 percent of all Americans saved less than 5 percent of their annual household income. Sixteen percent saved between 5 and 10 percent. Only nine percent saved more than 20 percent of their annual income. The average personal savings rate is now less than 2 percent of income. The average household has a net worth of just $264,000 at retirement, not including home equity.

The American Savings Education Council's 2004 report, "Saving and Retirement in America," stated that, among all workers, 45 percent have less than $25,000 in savings and investments (aside from equity in primary residences). According to a 2002 survey by the Consumer Federation of America, 25 percent of American households have net assets of less than $10,000.
According to Hewitt Associates, nearly half of all retirement plan participants who change jobs fail to roll over their accounts. They take the money instead, incurring unnecessary taxes and penalties for doing so.[37] In the December 2004 issue of Money, it was reported that another 25 percent have outstanding loans or have taken withdrawals on the job.

The United States is the richest country in the world, but we have the highest percentage of people living from paycheck to paycheck. As reported in "Escape the Credit Card Trap" in the October 6, 2005, issue of Kiplinger, a recent study from AC Nielsen revealed that about one in every four Americans say they don't have any spare cash.

In The Total Money Makeover, Dave Ramsey cited the Wall Street Journal as reporting that 70 percent of Americans live paycheck to paycheck. He also cited a poll from Parenting magazine stating that 49 percent of Americans could cover less than one month's expenses if they lost their income.

A recent study by the Levy Economics Institute found that, in 1999, nearly 42 percent of all American households were in asset poverty, that is, the family did not have enough in accessible financial assets to support itself for at least three months. Additionally, the report estimated that 46 percent of American households had less than $5,000 in liquid assets. (A liquid asset, in this case, includes IRAs, whose actual liquidity is debatable.)[38]

Other startling information about Americans in debt includes:
- According to an article posted on CNN/Money on October 12, 2005, the average credit card debt per household reached a record $9,312 in 2004. That's an increase of 116 percent over the past ten years.
- According to a report aired on Frontline on November 23, 2004, approximately 60 percent of Americans revolve balances. The average revolving balance, among individuals with at least one credit card, is now $3,815. Approximately 35 million Americans pay only the required minimum — as low as 2 percent — of their balance each month.
- According to "Credit Check," an article published in the September 2004 issue of Money, a United States public interest research group study found that 25 percent of consumer credit reports contained errors serious enough to lead to a denial of credit.

Debt can be a consuming fire. It can destroy everything around it, including marriages, friendships, health, and employment opportunities. Bad debt can also work internally to destroy your dreams and motivation. Unlike developing countries where access to credit is limited, in the United States, most people have more credit than they need because of the availability of credit. Just the thought of incorporating an enterprise into the mix during a time of debt seems ludicrous. But did I say incorporate? One of the doors out of debt can be through business incorporation. At one time, the person with the highest debt ratio in America was Ted Turner. He even filed for bankruptcy. But he was an entrepreneur, so no one talked negatively about him. In fact, he was—and is still—one of the most highly respected businessmen in the world.

What's good about debt? Almost everyone has some level of debt. Debt and lack of access to conventional banking services for small businesses is one of the reasons the industry of microenterprise was created. Even if you are in debt, you can use several national financial resources to build a small business. One of the best national organizations in the country that provides access to capital for entrepreneurs is ACCION USA, a private nonprofit organization that offers small business loans of up to $25,000 and financial literacy education to small business owners in the United States. ACCION USA has offices across the country as well as online access to the business loan application process. To find out more information about ACCION USA and its services, visit their Web site (www.ACCIONUSA.org).

Other providers of Internet-based loans for small business include www.kiva.org, www.prosper.com, and www.count-me-in.com. Both Kiva.org and Prosper.com allow individuals who need money for a business to submit their requests. Other people bid on the privilege of lending it to them. All three of these lenders were created internationally first and now make their services available in the United States.

Debt is an obstacle, but it is not insurmountable. Creating another income stream, a small business, is one way to pay debt. You can use the profits from your business to pay bad debts. Of course, you can always take a second job to pay your bills. But doesn't it feel better to think of ways to be profitable and productive through your own business instead?

Lemonade Success Story:
SUSAN'S STORY

Susan held a bachelor's degree in business administration and a master's degree in public administration. She was excited about her first job opportunities, but she was astonished to see that she had amassed more than $60,000 in student loans. Every entry-level position she had would not allow her the opportunity to pay off her student loan, and she continued to find herself in loan default. Susan decided she had to do something, so she started a small, Internet-based business on eBay. She became a power seller distributing hip-hop clothing and other products online. Over the last three years, she has paid off over half of her student loan debt. She enjoys the business so much that she is considering expanding her product line of clothing to retail stores.

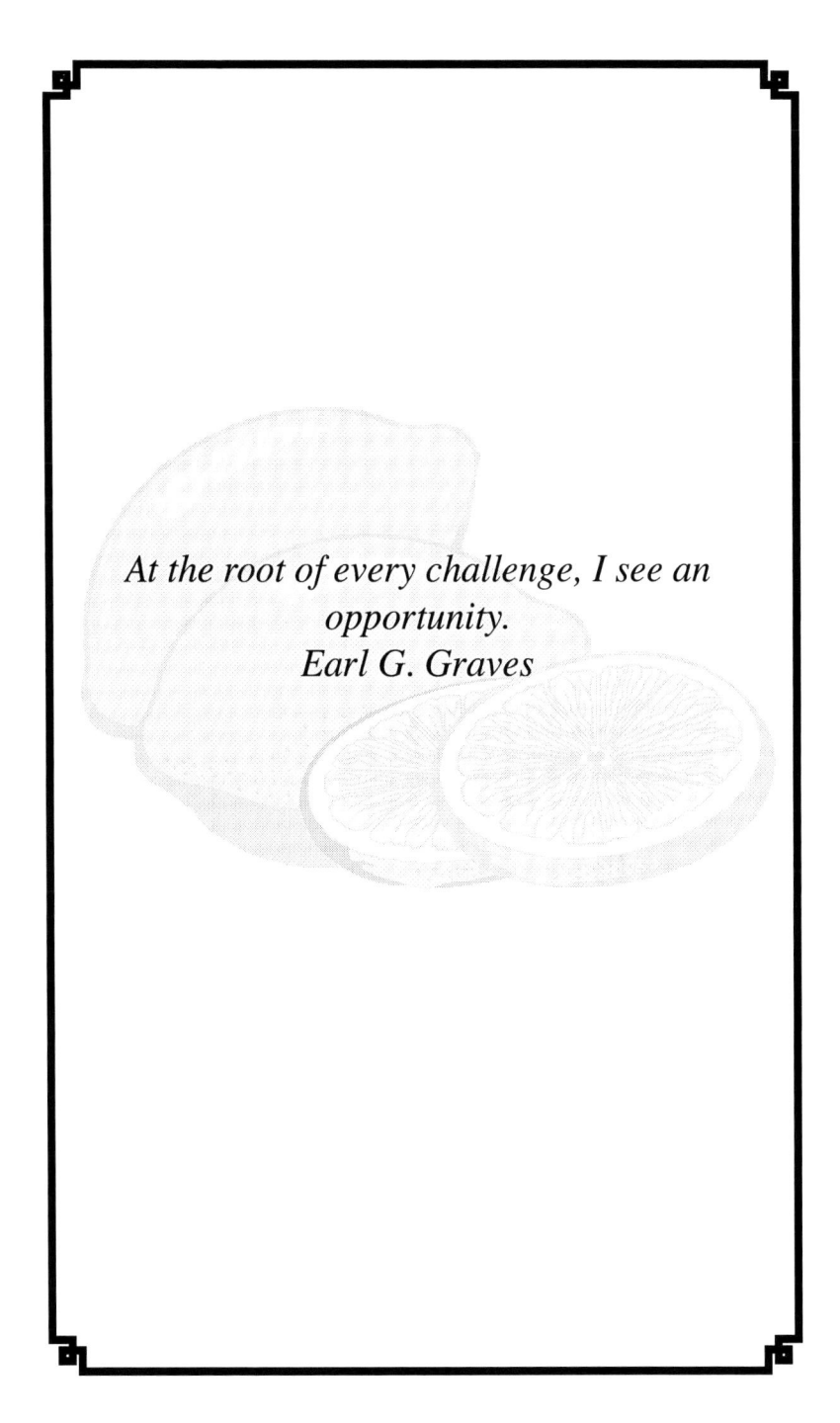

At the root of every challenge, I see an opportunity.
Earl G. Graves

Lemon # 5
Natural Disasters

Not since the Titanic has water been the center of destruction heard around the world. Like the Titanic, class was a major factor in who survived and how there were able to survive afterwards. Hurricane Katrina washed away a sense of independence for families. Evacuees were panicking because of the constant deadlines to file papers with the government and insurance companies to receive aid. Small, local companies desperate for cash flow in the wake of the storm are having trouble collecting on their business interruption insurance.

While people have finally identified and buried their relatives, they are still trying to reconnect their disconnected families. The lemons just keep on coming.

Since the days of slavery, there has never been a human disaster like Hurricane Katrina in the African American community that has been as devastating. Property, businesses, homes, and churches were lost. People lost their lives. Loans were due. Trained employees scattered. Seasonal businesses suffered. Everything was gone.

Now what? Hurricane Katrina fatigue has kicked in. People

don't want to hear your story anymore. Mardi Gras was held a few months after the storm. Business has taken precedence. Believe it or not, business works. While the government and other agencies continue to bring it together, you still need cash.

At a town hall session for Hurricane Katrina survivors, the auditorium was packed with upset people asking questions for the mayor and FEMA agents.

Where were the venders? Where were the entrepreneurs? I was astonished at what I saw. No one had a cart selling "I survived Katrina" T-shirts or local cuisine. There were no artists on the street. No one was making masks, and no one was writing down their thoughts. No one saw the opportunity to make money from such a large market.

One way for people to move forward is to concentrate on something that provides hope for tomorrow. Create a lemonade stand. Develop a product that people will demand. It is not impossible to see the possibilities. If all businesses in New Orleans were destroyed, they need to be rebuilt. They can be rebuilt and better. Former workers can now become owners.

It's an opportune time for those willing to go some business red tape to start businesses. For those who waded through mounds of documents, red tape, and agencies to get one check for $2,000 or a temporary VISA, you can do this. What's a little more paperwork? Now that you know the system, work it.

Americans need New Orleans and all it has to offer, including its music, food, people, and spirit. Rather than see the city destroyed, see the city as redistributed. This is a good time for survivors to plant, grow, and spread seeds to develop portable businesses. This message needs to be spread in churches, hotels, beauty parlors, social service agencies, and other places where survivors gather. The option of business development, even small ones, is critical at this crucial stage in their life. Everyone should have a résumé and business plan always at the ready and never be caught off guard again.

The expansion and creation of business opportunities for survivors is a crucial strategy to move people toward self-employment and possibly become self-sufficient. As newcomers to many areas, survivors are unfamiliar with business training opportunities. Few are encouraging them to find support through business ownership to increase their incomes and move toward self-sufficiency.

Merely obtaining employment after Hurricane Katrina is not the answer to eradicating the plight of many of the survivors. Small and micro business development will offer the survivors an opportunity for empowerment through ownership. By creating their own microenterprise, they decrease their reliance on other people and agencies. By owning their own micro business, they learn quickly that it will grow by working hard and putting effort into a small business of their own. Newly self-empowered micro business owners have a freedom. They have a self-sufficient awareness, a confidence their employed counterparts may not acquire. Survivors can receive business training, self-help counseling, and support from the business community to begin to rebuild and move forward. Business training programs can also provide information and referrals to access to business capitalization to help each business achieve greater economic success.

In every local economy, small business is important for creating job opportunities and improving economic vitality. The economy expands with every business contribution. Recent data indicated that small businesses with four or fewer employees annually create 43 percent of new jobs. [39]

Self-employment is a valid option for increasing the income of entrepreneurial people when they have support. Many Hurricane Katrina survivors who are emerging from their crisis can earn income and achieve economic independence through business ownership, but many larger or social service agencies are generally not aware of small business services available to aid them along that path. Possible portable businesses for survivors of disasters are hair stylist, florist, baker, artist, painter/wallpaper hanger, T-shirt vendor, musician, Web designer, pet groomer/trainer, personal trainer, caterer, picture framer, specialty cart owner, or real estate rehabber.

In the wake of Hurricane Katrina, displaced small and emerging businesses required access to financial capital to reestablish their business operations throughout Louisiana. Survivors who have returned can access several resources to find out more about business opportunities.

NewCorp Business Assistance Center (www.newcorpbac.net) provided a $2 million loan and equity capital fund to offer technical assistance and financing to all small and emerging businesses throughout the affected areas in Louisiana. This fund is not considered to be a disaster recovery fund. It is a business continuity fund. The fund will not attempt to replace uninsured business revenue and asset losses as a result of Hurricane Katrina. It will only focus on business reestablishments in areas within or outside of the affected areas. All applications for disaster recovery will be referred to the Small Business Administration and/or FEMA.

Good Work Network (GWN) (www.goodworknetwork.org) has been working since 2001 to promote micro-enterprise development in the New Orleans area. Since Hurricane Katrina, GWN has focused a large part of its efforts on child care providers, as 67 percent of day care facilities closed as a result of the storm.[40] It also works with individuals who already ran child care centers to help them think and act as business owners who could manage the financial and business aspects of their facilities professionally. The program aims to improve the quality of child care available in Louisiana and help the child care industry attract and retain highly qualified employees.

The Microenterprise Development Association of Louisiana (MEDAL) (www.microenterprisela.org) is a statewide association headquartered in Baton Rouge, but it provides business support services and training to community-based organizations who want to help individuals start businesses.

If you are a Hurricane Katrina survivor, these are a few of the support services available. Believe it or not, there are well-wishers and supporters across the country. The world is rooting for you and the city of New Orleans. If you doubt this, give it a try. Put out your lemonade cart. Revive or start your business. The country is in your corner. We are waiting for you to tell your story of survival through your product. Add a bit of New Orleans flavor to every location. Begin to grow where you are planted.

Lemonade Success Story:
LORETTA'S STORY

New Orleans candy maker Loretta Harrison had been selling pralines and other sugary treats at the New Orleans French Market for more than fifteen years before Hurricane Katrina shut down her business.

The storm dispersed, not deterred, Ms. Loretta. She knew she could continue her business. With her customers and employees scattered across the country, she restarted in Baton Rouge with the support of her immediate family. After many months of renovations, Ms. Loretta finally returned to live in her New Orleans home while renovations are underway. She began to sell her candy out of a warehouse in the Faubourg Marigny, just east of the French Quarter.

Her signature items include pralines, praline cookies, fudge, tomato bread, and sweet potato cookies.

"Everything is indigenous to here," she said. "Pralines came right into the market by slaves. These are old products. It's just like the red beans and rice and gumbo. It makes New Orleans what it is. We can't forget it."

*Pick yourself up, dust yourself off
and start all over again*
Dorothy Fields

Lemon # 6
Your Past

We sometimes find ourselves in an internal prison, an emotional prison. For women, sometimes it starts out being called "fast" as a little girl. This designation can progress to being easy to trifling to whorish. The final vernacular, in common terms today, would be "skank." A life of early sexual experiences to a progression of skankiness would be a lemon. Not having respect for one's own body can turn a woman into a commodity, something that can be bought and sold for little or nothing. Prostitution, strip clubs, adult movies, and Internet porn sites are all skank producers. The list of illicit moneymaking activities goes on and on. Though each of these activities can be considered entrepreneurial, they would also be considered lemons. Being physically washed up at thirty leaves a person with few options.

What can you do? Many women stay in the skank life because they feel they have no choice. Once pimped, always pimped. But the lemonade stand experience teaches you to take the same materials that life has thrown your way and turn them into profitable, legitimate businesses. By breaking down the components of skankiness, the features are the same for any business. Market or identify the product. Sell at a profitable price. Create an in-demand product. Be focused on the customer. Follow the trends.

There are skank success stories, including Traci Lords (from porn to legitimate movies), Eve (from stripper to rapper to actress), and Ice T (from former pimp to rapper to actor).

The movie Hustle and Flow chronicles the story of two prostitutes and a pimp. One prostitute uses her singing ability to reach beyond prostitution to entrepreneurship. The other uses business skills, sales, and promotion to move from whoredom to rapper, producer, and business manager. The pimp used his pimp ways to become a rapper. Only in America can you go from skank to success through entrepreneurship.

I believe that living on the edge, living in and through your fear, is the summit of life, and that people who refuse to take that dare condemn themselves to a life of living death.
John H. Johnson

Lemon # 7
Death

Death is a lemon. Death of a loved one stops you dead in your tracks, sometimes for years. You spend time agonizing over your own loss of their presence. You keep dwelling over the issues and unfinished business. You think about all the kind words that were left unspoken and all the kind deeds that were left undone. Even with all the words from well-wishers, nothing matters except the grief. That hole in the middle of your being is still there. It may not, as some say, go away with time. Time does heal all wounds, but grief is not a wound. It is a reality.

In Signs, the director included a scene that depicted the senseless death of the preacher's wife. The incident occurred because of a tragic coincidence. A man fell asleep while driving a truck, which ran into the wife while she was taking an evening stroll. The preacher's wife was killed, causing the preacher to give up his faith and profession. He was left with only his wife's final words, "see" and "swing away." He thought her words were useless brain sparks. He questioned God, and his belief in goodness and righteousness faded. Later, the movie unveiled the everyday signs and miracles. Signs are with us. When the time is right, they will show up for us.

Death is a sign of something ending, but it is also a sign of a new beginning. The passing of my mother motivated me to complete this book and concentrate more on my own writing. I had always written in a journal. I had kept one since I learned how to write, but my writing became more intense and less fulfilling. It could not fill the gaping hole of grief in my life. I thought the best way for me to move forward was to write more deliberately, helping myself and others in the process. This book project is now one of a series of guides I am developing to help others navigate their way out of despair through productive activities.

One of the best things you can honor a loved one's passing is to create something that will continue to live on and be productive. Some people plant trees. Others set up foundations and endowments. Those are wonderful ideas, but you can create a business enterprise and dedicate it to the memory of your loved one. Every time you serve a customer, create a new product, employ someone, or fulfill a need, think of how you are giving back to others a bit of what has been invested in you. A business can be passed down from generation to generation. It is a wonderful gift to give and leave behind.

Sugar

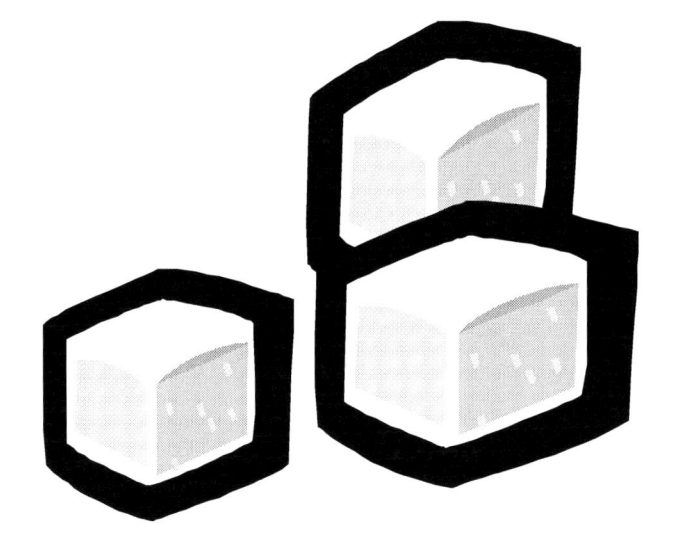

Sweet man-made resources

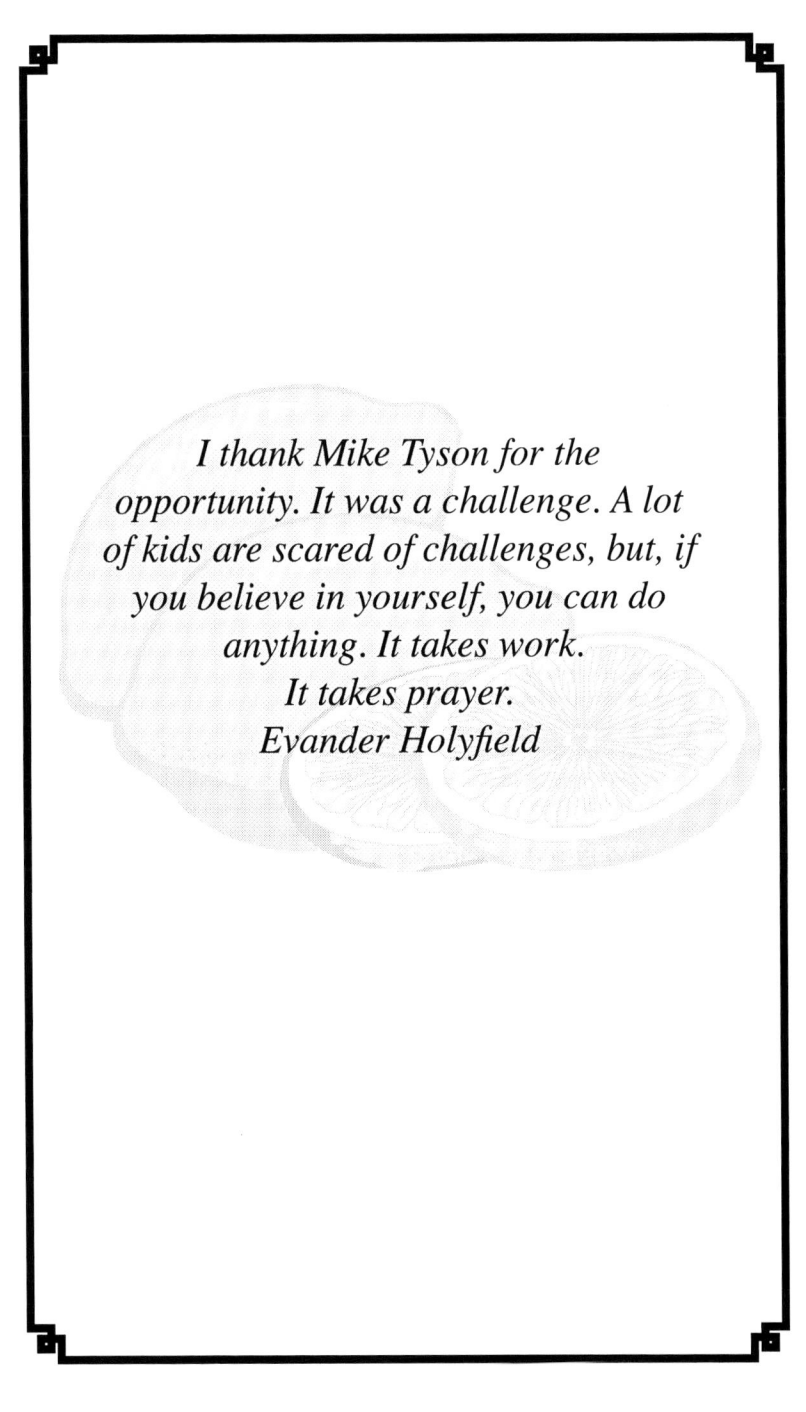

I thank Mike Tyson for the opportunity. It was a challenge. A lot of kids are scared of challenges, but, if you believe in yourself, you can do anything. It takes work.
It takes prayer.
Evander Holyfield

Turn Your Woe into Dough

When it cannot get any worse, what do you do? To me, "woe" describes a sorry state of affairs, that is, a distinct sadness. But it is also a time to stop and think. Reflect on the situation. One of the best things about developing a business idea is that it comes from a thought. It is an observation of a needed product or service.

Stop and think about what you can do right now to make some money. What if you had to do it quickly and had no way to borrow it? What would you do? Some of the best thoughts come during these times. Lack sets off certain survival instincts in the human brain. Pause to consider and hear what speaks to you. You may have considered these thoughts before, but you were busy or not in a state of woe.

If you have a journal, this is the time to write. The Lemonade Business Journal was created to help you think through the process of making dough. You can also use any other brainstorming tools to help you open your mind to enterprise possibilities. Better yet, it will help you return to some of the creative places you visited or creative ventures you considered at an earlier time in your life.

What did you want to be when you grew up? Some might have said entrepreneur, but Americans are not taught to think this way at an early age. Teachers, educational institutions, case managers, parole officers, vocational guidance counselors, and well-meaning family and friends tend to steer us toward the safety of traditional employment activities. A few people were introduced to business and market concepts early in life. Even fewer actually participated in entrepreneurship classes during their formal years of education.

Entrepreneurship can be taught, but it does not have to be. Better yet, it can be experienced. Exposure to entrepreneurial activities is actually a better indicator of future success in business ventures. Most entrepreneurs were introduced to entrepreneurship by their parents.

One indicator of entrepreneurial success is watching other entrepreneurs at work. Immigrants will often staff their establishments with their children, who learn how to make change, serve customers, and develop products at an early age. Rather than thinking as consumers, they think as producers.

When I was in grade school, I and a few of my friends sold our lunches to others. We used the money to buy candy and fund the theatrical productions we regularly gave in my parents' garage.

I'm a sucker for the kids selling candy and magazines on the street because that's where the entrepreneurial skills start."
Leon Jackson

Opening a Lemonade Stand Is Easy

Inc. magazine ran an interesting contest to identify "the best lemonade stand in America." The contest was open to kids between the ages of five and twelve. The goal was to seek out and acknowledge young entrepreneurs who took creative approaches to developing lemonade stands and ran their stand in an exemplary manner. Inc. writers and readers selected the winners. The summer's grand prize winner was scheduled to receive a $1,000 savings bond.

If a child can do it, can it be so difficult? Actually starting a business is easier than it seems. People do it every day, especially people with few options. For some, entrepreneurship is the only choice, not just the best choice for their economic survival and self-sufficiency.

In America, business development has been placed on an almost unattainable pedestal. Requirements for a startup business fill pages and pages of books. People think they have to fill out complicated forms and make complex decisions to start a small business.

Is all of this necessary? Not really. Most importantly, you need to first identify a product or service that you can sell for a profit. Everything else is gravy. Big business is hard, costly, time-consuming, and difficult. Small business is not. You can grow a small business into a big business with experience, drive, and a good product. As you learn more about business, you will be able to apply these principles along the way as your business grows.

Recent studies indicate that self-employment is on the rise. Demographics and economic factors are driving the surge in self-employment, creating optimism that the overall economy will continue to grow. In an economy in which many big businesses are struggling, small businesses are not. Creating small enterprises is an important factor in increasing job opportunities and improving economic vitality. The economy expands with new business created.

Small enterprises are a critical component of community and economic development. According to a recent study sponsored by the United States Small Business Administration, self-employment rates are on the rise across the country. The report indicated that Internet start-ups, minorities, women, and baby boomers are driving the surge.[41] Baby boomers are looking for more security later in life as large corporations continue to downsize and buy out senior staff members. Recent data showed that the number of self-employed people over the age of fifty has jumped 23 percent since 1990 to 5.6 million workers.[42]

New figures from the United States Census Bureau confirm what many experts have long suspected. The United States is in the midst of a major boom in self-employment. Data from 2004 showed that 19.5 million Americans are self-employed, and their numbers are growing. Between 2003 and 2004, the number of self-employed grew by one million, about 4.7 percent.[43]

Internet retailers have contributed to the increased small business creation. Other Internet communities that create seamless communication and selling tools are also on the rise. Online shopping tools, like PayPal, have also made Internet-based selling an attractive and affordable way to open a small business.
According to the Small Business Administration, women now comprise 32 percent of the country's business owners, up from 25 percent in 1983. Hispanics, African Americans, and Asians also made strong gains in self-employment in the past two years.[44]

"Self-employment is critical to our economy," said Thomas M. Sullivan, chief counsel for advocacy at the Small Business Administration. "The increase in self-employment rates for women, blacks, and Latinos show that small business ownership can move minorities and women further into our economic mainstream."

A recent poll in USA Today conducted by VISA/Score featured a lemonade stand and noted the top challenges for very small business owners was their inability to focus on generating new business. Of the 1,000 entrepreneurs surveyed, one-third chose this category as most challenging. Other challenges sited in the survey were spreading time across multiple projects and roles (27 percent), limited resources (23 percent), the need to run the business more efficiently (23 percent), and not having enough time to focus on passions (23 percent).[45]

> ## *Lemonade Success Story:*
> ## A Piece of Cake
>
> Melissa Bunnen is the founder and president of A Piece of Cake, a multimillion dollar cake delivery business. Melissa said she was not a good cook when she opened her business. Rather, she was an excellent observer who noted the flower delivery business to corporate American was booming. Why not extend the business to another product? She identified good cake recipes and began baking from her home kitchen. Within a few years, she had grown her business to be a million-dollar enterprise with a free-standing warehouse in an upscale part of Atlanta.

It's okay to start small. Stop making excuses. Just start. Procrastination cuts into profits. You can even start at the smaller than small business level, the micro level. In the United States, most businesses actually start at the micro level. Many grow, but they sometimes remain the patch of income that you can count on to get you through the rough places. Many micro businesses are mobile and transferable. They follow you where you go.

How do you start the process? Easy! Think: What you do now that you enjoy? What do you do that comes naturally? What are your hobbies? What do you do in your spare time? What do you do well? What comes easily for you? In what area do you receive the most compliments? What makes you smile? What have you done repeatedly and still enjoy?

Consider the following. What do people need? What do people enjoy? What would make life easier for someone else? How can you help? What would others be willing to pay for what can you sell well? What type of business can you start now? What business enterprise will help you make some money now?

Starting a small business requires a certain amount of preparation. You can make your first steps small. Take time to think through a clear vision to help you get started. Have you ever sold anything? If so, you are way ahead of many of the business plan entrepreneurs, people who spend all of their time writing about business and planning for one but never actually run an outfit or sell items. If you have ever sold anything to anyone or provided services to customers, you are well on your way to being a successful entrepreneur.

Change your mind. It is very possible to change your mind without changing your situation, parentage, or life circumstances. It's your mind. If you want, change it. Start dropping entrepreneurial thoughts into it. The Bible says in the book of Proverbs 23:7, "As a man thinketh, so is he." You can begin to read, write, and envelop yourself in the essence of entrepreneurship.

Identify locations where entrepreneurs gather. Check out the research section of the local library. Read the books and magazines that entrepreneurs read. Read entrepreneurial biographies. Better yet, read biographies and see the entrepreneur in person.

Businesses grow best in networks of similar businesses because they face similar constraints. If you market to similar customers and work together to solve constraints, you can reach more customers.

Before the industrial revolution came to American, most men and women were landowners and entrepreneurs. Before the great migration to Northern cities to work in factories, people made money from their skills, hands, trades, and ingenuity. You can change your choice of words when you're out in the world when you describe yourself as a businessperson. Talk about your business proudly, whether it is a start-up or not. Treat it like it is a business, not like it's about to be a business. Don't say, "I'm trying to start a business." That sounds noncommittal. Even if you've only printed your own business cards, say, "I own my own business" or "I'm a consultant." This will help you think of yourself as an entrepreneur.

Entrepreneurship is challenging, but taking advantage of business training services, technical assistance, financial resources, and support networks in your community can take out some of the sour and begin the sweetening process.

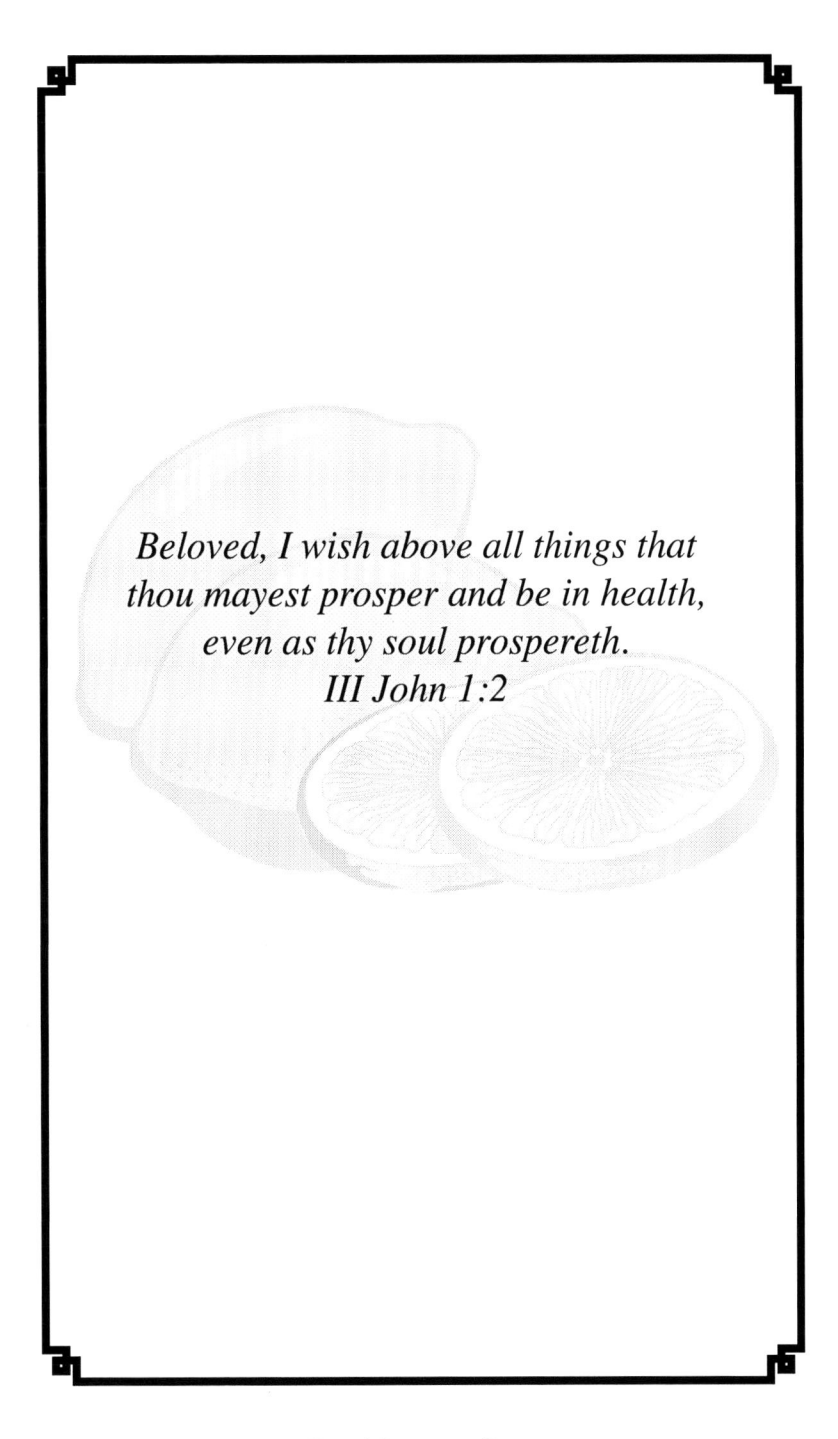

Beloved, I wish above all things that thou mayest prosper and be in health, even as thy soul prospereth.
III John 1:2

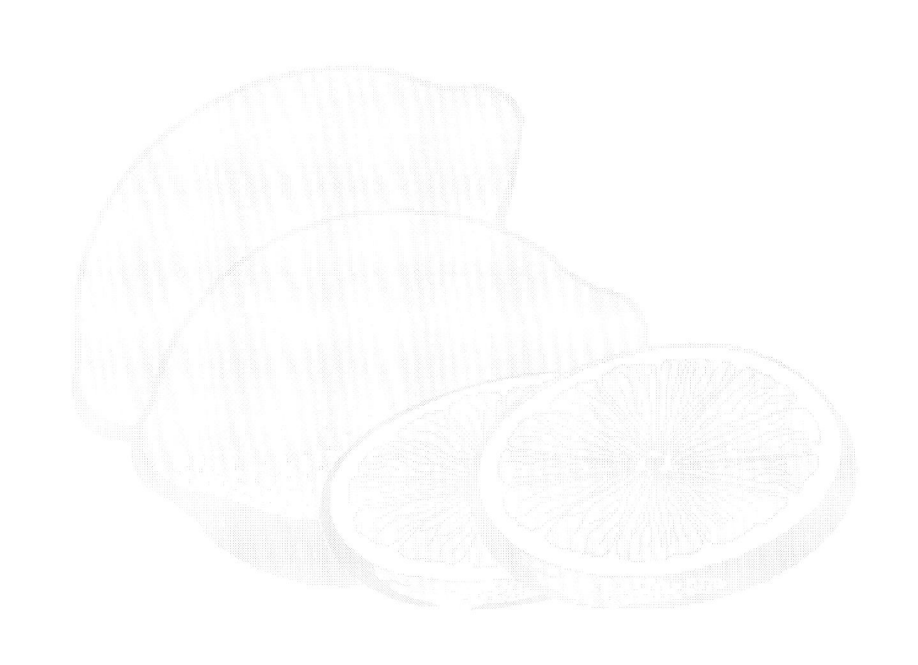

Biblical Lemonade Stands

Lemons have been around a long time. I wouldn't be surprised if that was a lemon tree in the Garden of Eden rather than an apple tree. Mankind has had to deal with challenges, deviations, and devastations for quite some time. Even in biblical days, there was quite a bit of lemonade stand activity happenings. Several biblical life stories with an entrepreneurial twist include:

- **Joseph:** Joseph was sold into slavery by his brothers. Falsely accused, he went to jail. While in jail, he honed his management and dream interpretation skills. While he was away, his gift made room for him. He used his abilities to become a business consultant to the pharaoh. Joseph, an ex-offender, saved his brothers, their families, and his people from famine.
- **Moses:** Moses was a hit-and-run murderer. While he was on the run, he developed leadership skills while hiding out in the wilderness. He used those skills to lead his people through the wilderness and brought them to the edge of the land that was promised to them.
- **The Widow of the Son of the Prophet:** She needed quick cash to pay her debts to keep her sons out of slavery. She went to the prophet, Elisha and he, asked her what she had in her house. She told him she only had one pot of oil He blessed

her resource and gave her good advice also, to go into the oil business. As long as she poured oil into her available vessels, it continued to flow until she filled up all the many borrowed vessels with oil. She sold all the oil and kept her sons out of bondage and slavery.
- **Peter, James, and John:** These marginal fishermen became the most successful fishers of men in history.
- **Jesus Christ:** Wood was used to make his cross. He took the cross, turned it into a crown, and brought the story of salvation to the entire world.

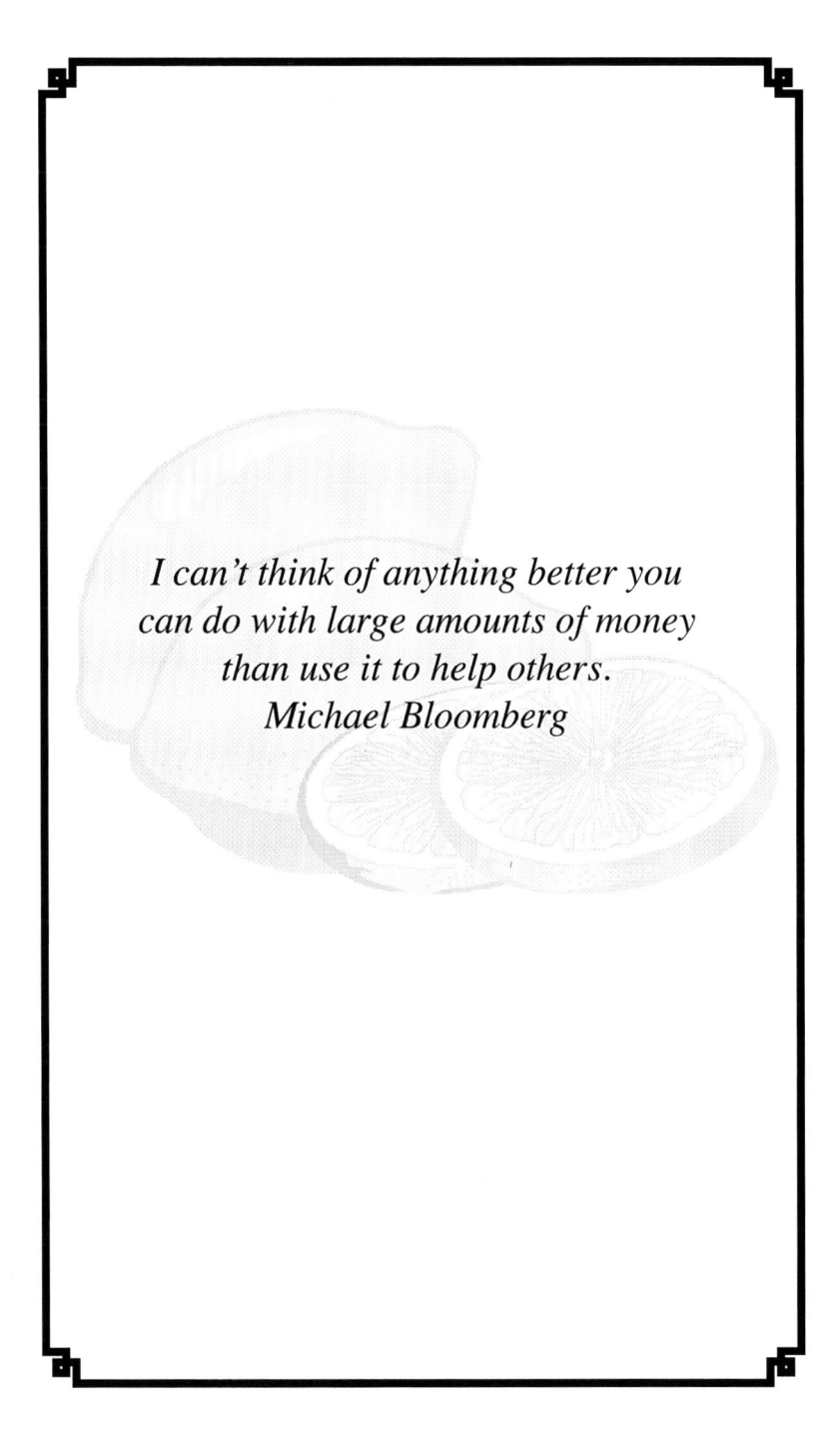

I can't think of anything better you can do with large amounts of money than use it to help others.
Michael Bloomberg

When Life Gives You Lemons

Lemonaires

In America, you can make it even with a lemon on your shoulder. Stories of entrepreneurial success abound, but we sometimes don't know even the greatest, wealthiest, and best-known entrepreneurs have made it despite one lemon or another. More than 75 percent of the adults in the United States lack a college degree.[46] The percentage of American high school graduates that start college is only 66 percent. The majority, 58 percent, of students who start a four-year degree program never finish.[47] A college degree and formal education are the benchmark for success, but, strangely, many of the most successful entrepreneurs don't have degrees. The Pennylicious Blog notes that more than 100 members of the Forbes 400 wealthiest Americans in 2006 never graduated from college or graduated long after they reached success in their businesses . The "lemonaires list" includes:
- Bill Gates and Paul Allen (Microsoft founders)
- Michael Dell (Dell Computer founder)
- Larry Ellison (Oracle founder)
- Norm and Theodore Waitt (Gateway Computer founder)
- Richard M. DeVos (Amway founder)
- Steve Jobs (Apple Computer founder)
- Thomas Monaghan (Domino's Pizza founder)

- Jim Jannard (Oakley Sunglasses founder)
- Ernest Gallo (Gallo wineries)
- Leonard Riggio (Barnes & Noble CEO)
- Bob Pittman (MTV founder)
- Micky Arison (Carnival Cruise Lines)
- David Geffen (music industry)
- Jay Van Andel (Amway)
- John Glenn (astronaut/senator)
- Ralph Lauren (fashion designer)
- Rosie O'Donnell (actress/talk show host)
- Wolfgang Puck (restaurateur)
- Ted Turner (media entrepreneur)
- Marilyn vos Savant (columnist)
- Wayne Huizenga (Blockbuster Video founder)
- Peter Jennings (ABC News anchor)
- Walter Cronkite (journalist/news anchor)
- Harry S. Truman (president)
- Debra Fields (Mrs. Fields)
- Sean Combs (music/fashion mogul)
- Russell Simmons (music/fashion mogul)
- Steve Chen (YouTube cofounder)

You don't need a college degree to start a business, get a business license, or run a successful, profitable business. Lemonaires made it happen without degrees. You can, too!

Lemonade Stands

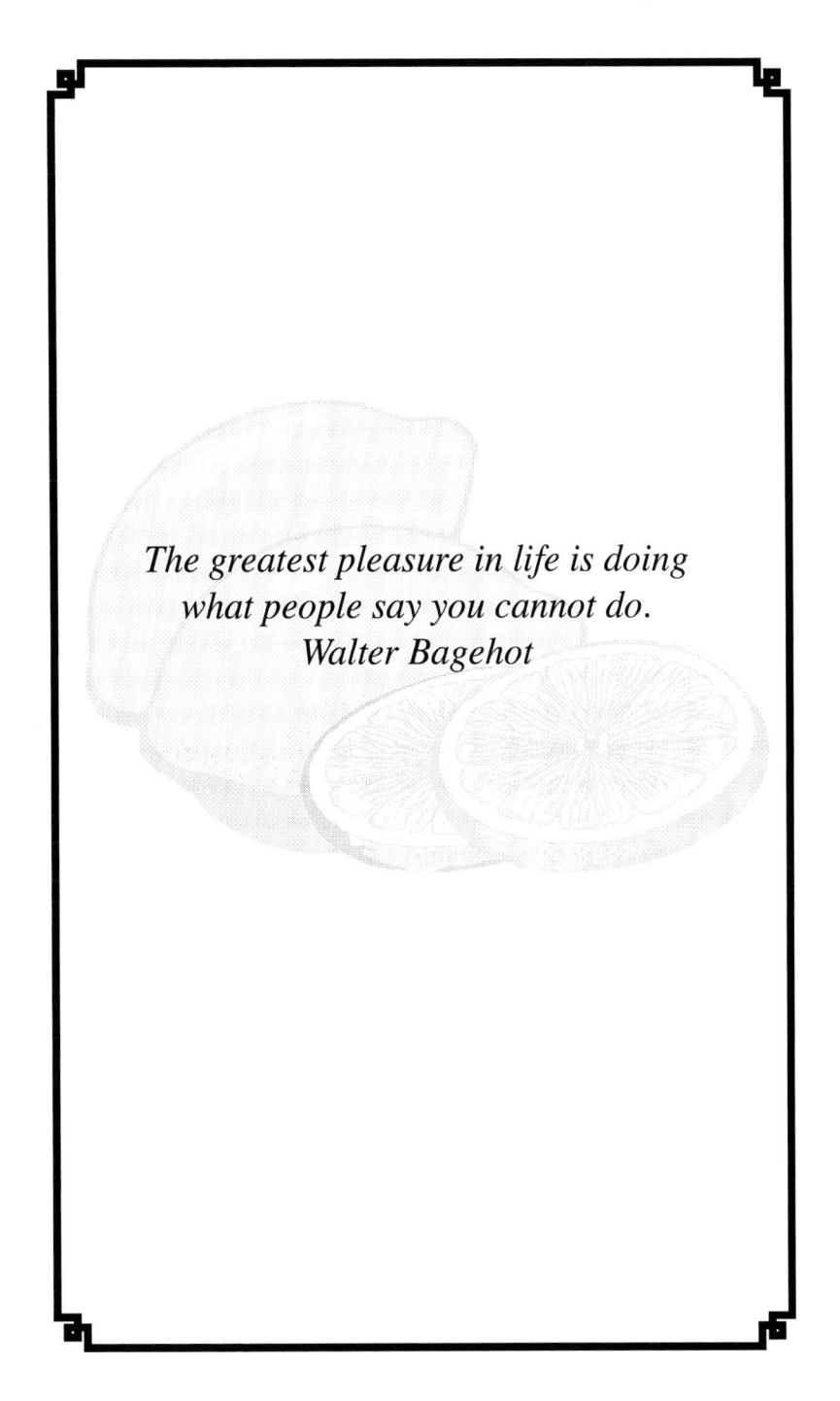

The greatest pleasure in life is doing what people say you cannot do.
Walter Bagehot

Lemonade Stands for Everybody!

What if all of us had small businesses? It's not such a crazy thought. The majority of the developing world is comprised of entrepreneurs who run small businesses. In developing countries, entrepreneurship is the economic vehicle that supports the family. Many children learn to entrepreneurship at the feet of their parents and gain business skills while working in the family enterprise. Countries without traditional industries tend to be more supportive of new start-ups and do not discourage the creation of small businesses that sell products and services. Can you imagine what would happen if you opened a fruit stand on an average corner in America? The police would stop by and ask you for a license, registration, permit, and so forth. There are more obstacles to start a business in our less entrepreneurial-friendly society, but businesses still start every day.

If your life has been lemoned, you can still make it a good, profitable, and worthy life. We have explored various avenues and ways to turn adventures into ventures, pick up life's broken pieces, turn them into financial mosaics, and potentially view the busted and disgusted pieces of our lives as possible business opportunities. Why not decide from this day forward to produce all you can, while you can, and turn every day into a sweet, productive day? The next time life gives you a lemon, squeeze it until it turns sweet.

Upcoming Books & Publications

The Lemonade Stand Series: Volume II

The second volume of this book will deal with the following additional life lemons: age, sexual orientation, literacy, illegal immigrant status, HIV/AIDS, single parenthood, and homelessness.

Upcoming Publications

The Lemonade Stand Journal
The Lemonade Stand Business Plan
The Lemonade Stand Resource Guide
Imitation of Life: Why White Women are More Successful in Business than African American Women (March 2008)
The 60-Minute Business Plan
Growing Up COGIC: How Holiness Can Lead to Success and Happiness (December 2007)

Co-Author
Young, Gifted, and Entrepreneurial:
Success Stories of the Prudential Young Entrepreneur Program: Volume 1

Workshops by Elizabeth Wilson

EW & Associates will tailor workshops and seminars to meet your needs. Samples presentations:

Business Development
When Life Gives You Lemons, Open a Lemonade Stand
Economic and Business Development in the 21st Century
The 60-Minute Business Plan
From Your Kitchen to the Store: How to Sell What You Make
Releasing Your Entrepreneurial Spirit
Credit: Repairs, Realities, and Rip-Offs
Chicken Dinners and Beyond: Unique Strategies for Church Economic Development
Business Planning by the Book
Entrepreneurial Training for the Multicultural Market
Finding Success in Corporate America
Small Business Boot Camp

Empowerment
The Rules by the Book
Single, Saved, and Satisfied
Okay, God, Where is My Spouse?
Dressing for Success for Less
Cheap Chic: Living the Life You Love
Finding Success in a Global Economy
Chariots of Fire
Feet

Onyx Publishing Company

ORDER FORM

Billing Name:
Name: _____
Address: _____
City: _____ State: _____ Zip: _____
Phone: (_____) _____

Shipping Info:
Name: _____
Address: _____
City: _____ State: _____ Zip: _____
Phone: (_____) _____

Item	Qty	Price	Total
When Life Gives You Lemons Open a Lemonade Stand	____	$14.99	_____
Tax			_____
Shipping		2.50	_____
Total Due			$_____

Payment Type: ○ Check   ○ Money Order   ○ Cash

Mail Form/Checks to: Elizabeth Wilson
3695F Cascade Road, Suite #1124
Atlanta, Georgia 30331-2105

www.elizabethwwilson.com

Contact Us

For further information:

Elizabeth W. Wilson
EW & Associates, Inc.
3695F Cascade Road, Suite #1124
Atlanta, Georgia 30331-2105

www.elizabethwwilson.com

(404) 344-2601 (Voice)
(404) 344-2599 (Fax)

About the Author

Elizabeth Williams-Wilson has provided professional leadership and training in the development of nonprofit services and management, including program design, project planning, staff recruitment, marketing and fund-raising. Elizabeth developed the first microenterprise program for women in Atlanta, BusinessNOW. She and was instrumental in founding, organizing, and coordinating the Georgia Microenterprise Network, the trade association for microenterprise programs in Georgia.

An entrepreneur, professional speaker, and owner of EW & Associates, Inc., Elizabeth has worked tirelessly to provide entrepreneurial training opportunities for the disadvantaged and disabled. She has trained hundreds of community-based organizations around the country, working with microentrepreneurs on economic literacy, youth entrepreneurship, small business development, and women's empowerment. She has also assisted low-income women and disadvantaged individuals in developing small businesses and reaching self-sufficiency. Elizabeth continues to be actively involved in her community and beyond by making presentations to organizations, coalitions, churches, and associations. She also provides consulting services to several women's international economic development organizations.

Elizabeth is a self-proclaimed "profitess," corporate trainer, and award-winning communications professional. Her oratorical skills were honed at the feet of her father, her minister and mentor, who taught her to use her gifts to empower other people's lives.

[1] Readers Digest, http://www.rd.com/content/extraordinaryuses/extraordinary-uses-for-lemons/

[2] U.S. Bureau of the Census, Survey of Income and Participation (1997) Disabilities Affect on Fifth of All Americans. Census brief: http://www.census.govprod/3/97pubs/cenbr975PDF

[3] Ibid

[4] Ibid

[5] Wenger B. Kaye, S & LaPlante, M. (1996) Disability Among Children. Disability Statis-tics

[6] Cornucopia of Disability Information, Disability Statistics [No Pity, Joe Shapiro], 1992

[7] Ibid

[8] U.S. Census Bureau, Facts for Features, July 1, 2006

[9] Americans with Disabilities Report, www.census.gov/press re-lease/www.releases/archives/

[10] Cornucopia of Disability Information, Disability Statistics [No Pity, Joe Shapiro], 1992

[11] Homicide among young black males—United States, 1978–1987. MMWR Morb Mortal Wkly Rep. 1990;39: 869–873.

[12] Cornucopia of Disability Information, Disability Statistics [No Pity, Joe Shapiro], 1992

[13] Diabetes in African Americans Fact Sheet, National Diabetes Information National In-stitute of Diabetes, Digestive and Kidney Diseases

[14] Ibid

[15] Ibid

[16] Ibid

[17] Ibid

[18] Arnold, Nancy L. Economic Development & Self Employment: A Status Report on Re-habilitation Activities & Models Relevant to Vocational Rehabilitation and Independent Living, Rural Facts, Missoula The University of Montana, Rural Institute

[19] Nelson, Candace (Editor) The Aspen Institute in collaboration with the Association for Enterprise Opportunity Fact Sheet Series, Microenterprise Development in the United States, An Overview, Issue #1 Washington, DC, The Aspen Institute, Fall 2000

[20] Nancy Arnold, Nancy L. Economic Development & Self Employment: A Status Report on Rehabilitation Activities & Models Relevant to Vocational Rehabilitation and Inde-pendent Living, Rural Facts, Missoula The University of Montana, Rural Institute

[21] Ibid

[22] Family Violence Prevention Fund the Facts on Domestic Violence (http://www.endabuse.org/resources/facts/domestic violence. PDF)

[23] Ibid

[24] U.S. Census Bureau, Minority & Women-Owned Business Enterprises

[25] SCORE, Stats on Women in Business, http://www.SCORE.org/women.stats.html

[26] Else, John, with Gallagher, Janice. An Overview of the Microenterprise Development Field in the U.S. (Geneva: ILO, 2001)

[27] Ibid

[28] The Aspen Institute, Economic Opportunities Program, Microenterprise Assistance: What Are We Learning About Results? Key Findings from the Aspen Institute's Self-Employment Learning Project (Washington, D.C.: The Aspen Institute, November 1999)

[29] Office of Advocacy, U.S. Small Business Administration. "Redefining Business Success: Distinguishing Between Closure and Failure" Head, Brian. www.sba.gov/advo/stats/bh_sbe03.PDF

[30.] Else, John, with Gallagher, Janice. An Overview of the Microenterprise Development Field in the U.S. (Geneva: ILO, 2001)

[31.] Pager, Devah, 2003, "Mark of a Criminal Record" American Journal of Sociology, 108 (5): 937-975

[32.] Adams, Devon, Lara Reynolds, Bureau of Justice Statistics "2002: At A Glance" U.S. Department of Justice Programs Bureau of Justice Statistics, August 2002 NJC 19449

[33.] Ibid

[34.] Education and Employment: A Re-Entry Briefing Paper, "Outside the Walls: A Natural Snapshot of Community-based Prison Re-entry Programs, www.reentrymedia.outreach.org/pdfs/employment/bp/pdf

[35.] Office of Advocacy, U.S. Small Business Administration. "Redefining Business Success: Distinguishing Between Closure and Failure" Head, Brian. www.sba.gov/advo/stats/bh_sbe03.PDF

[36.] Putnam Investment Survey of the Working Retired, "Retirement Only a Breather: 7 Million Go Back to Work" December 8, 2005, http://www.putnam.com/survey.htm

[37.] Money, December 2004, page 94 It's Your Money, www.moneyspot.org

[38.] Carter, Asena, Wolff, Edward. Levy Economic Institute, 1999, Asset Poverty in the United States 1984 – 1999, Evidence from the Panel Study of Income Dynamic Working Papers/October 2002, Working Paper No. 356.

[39.] Small Business Administration, www.sba.gov/gopher/lesgislationandregulations/factadv.txt

[40.] Agenda for Children: Alerts, www.agendaforchildren.org/alerts/htm

[41.] SCORE, Counselors to American Small Business, small biz stats and trends, U.S. Small Business administration Office of Advocacy, AARP/Rand Corp. "Self-Employment and the 50 Population"

[42.] U.S. Census Bureau News, Press Release, July 2006

[43.] Ibid

[44] SCORE, Counselors to American Small Business, small biz stats and trends, U.S. Small Business administration Office of Advocacy, AARP/Rand Corp. "Self-Employment and the 50 Population"

[45] VISA News Release. "Sole-proprietors are happier on their own, but feel distracted, overwhelmed playing multiple roles" San Francisco, CA August 7, 2006

[46] The Atlantic, entitled, America's Forgotten Majority, 00.06 www.theatlantic.com/issues/2000/06/rogers.htm

[47] Ibid

[48] Pennylicious blog, "Billionaire Drop Outs" http://www.pennylicious.com/2006/10/09/billionaire-dropouts/